ID0983540

Harnessing the Strength of the World's
Most Powerful Management Philosophy

Servant-Leadership
Across
Cultures

Fons Trompenaars
and **Ed Voerman**

New York Chicago San Francisco Lisbon London Madrid Mexico City
Milan New Delhi San Juan Seoul Singapore Sydney Toronto

Library of Congress Cataloging-in-Publication Data

Trompenaars, Alfons.
    Servant-leadership across cultures : harnessing the strengths of the world's most powerful management philosophy / by Fons Trompenaars and Ed Voerman.
       p.   cm.
    Includes index.
    ISBN 978-0-07-166435-6 (alk. paper)
    1. Servant leadership.   I. Voerman, Ed.   II. Title.

  HM1261.T757   2010
  658.4'092—dc22   2009026008

There is a story told at Wharton University of a brilliant student from Mexico who ran out of money because of a financial crisis affecting his country. The day before this student had to give up his studies and return home, a scholarship opportunity miraculously appeared.

*Russ Ackoff, thank you for everything you have taught us.
You are a true servant-leader.*

Excerpts from *The Case for Servant Leadership* by Kent M. Keith, © Copyright Kent M. Keith 2008, reprinted by permission of the author. "The Paradoxical Commandments" by Kent M. Keith, © Copyright Kent M. Keith 1968, renewed 2001, reprinted by permission of the author.

1 2 3 4 5 6 7 8 9 10 11 12 13 14 15 16 17 18 19 20 21 22   WFR/WFR   0 9

ISBN 978-0-07-166435-6
MHID   0-07-166435-1

CONTENTS

128137

FOREWORD

In these times of ever more globalization, almost everyone is faced with culture differences in one way or another. This book offers a practical approach, based on the principles of servant-leadership, for how people can deal with these differences.

Both the authors have extensive international experience on which to draw. As an intercultural consultant, Fons Trompenaars has built up a database of more than 80,000 responses to questions about cultural differences during the last two decades. Ed Voerman both lived and worked in South America for eight years and has since led various international organizations.

As a result of coupling their international experience with the principles of servant-leadership, the authors have found several practical insights. For example, that servant-leaders are particularly skilled at building bridges between cultures, because with servant-leadership, there is no "us" and "them"; it is the shared goals that are important. Servant-leaders do not let themselves be tempted into making choices between opposing values, nor do they make dissatisfying compromises. Distinctive of the servant-leaders' approach is that they, where possible, choose a solution whereby opposing values or goals are combined in such a way that each actually strengthens the other.

The authors show that this leadership principle is not at all new by providing examples from ancient cultures such as those in Greece (Plato), China, and India. They have chosen seven important dilemmas to illustrate seven dimensions of cultural differences: leading-serving; rules-exceptions; parts–the whole; control-passion; specific-diffuse; short term–long term; push-pull.

The dilemmas clearly illustrate the kinds of issues that businesspeople can encounter when operating in an international context. The focus of this book is on the manner in which servant-leaders deal with dilemmas. This is explained using the example of Peter Webber, manager of a multinational enterprise.

This book is especially recommended for leaders who make decisions using their minds but who also want to work from the heart. They dare to ask themselves: "Who or what do I serve with this decision?" It is also meant for people who are active in a multicultural community; for people who have international contact on a daily basis; and those who are working globally, even for expats.

The authors' end conclusion is both positive and hopeful for the future; there are challenging cultural differences that can be overcome with the principle of servant-leadership. And, thankfully, people are not the same, but equal.

Herman Wijffels
World Bank, Washington
Director of the Board for the Greenleaf Foundation
September 2008

ACKNOWLEDGMENTS

Many people have contributed to the creation of this book.

For this English edition, we would like to thank the "three musketeers"—Barbara Blokpoel, Carolien Brinks, and Evi Collins—who, in the process of translating, implemented constructive changes to realize a completed English version within a tight time frame. Chapeau et merci.

For the Dutch version, we would also like to thank Henk den Dekker, recent graduate of the Servant-Leadership Academy, for his feedback and suggestions, and again Carolien Brinks for her tireless support and help with the different Dutch revisions. Finally, many thanks go to Petra Pronk for her work as Dutch editor and help in putting together the original version of the book.

All of you have lived the principles of servant-leadership in completing this project.

BACKGROUND

A recently merged multinational has its first meeting with its new management team. The Americans are full of anticipation, curious about their Japanese colleagues' opinion of the upcoming developments in the stock market. However, there is an uncomfortable stillness in the room. After several ever more desperate attempts to get the conversation going, there is an awkwardness hanging in the air. The Americans cannot understand why the Japanese refuse to open their mouths and get a conversation going, while the Japanese are at a loss as to why their new colleagues are being so confrontational.

Similar situations occur on a daily basis, all over the globe, wherever people work across cultures. In their own cultures, their modus operandi is the norm; it is considered socially acceptable, and, because of that, they never take a moment to consider that there might be other ways that are equally acceptable in other cultures—that is until they have an experience with a new colleague from some other part of the world, other organization, or other department, who does things in a completely foreign way. And the way their colleague does things is not only foreign but also, at least from their point of view, less optimal. Ironically, the new colleague is thinking the exact same thing about them. The result: a culture clash. This costs time, money, and a great deal of frustration. In the most extreme cases, these clashes can even mean the end of the organization.

This is a serious problem, especially because of the ever-increasing importance of cooperation in a world characterized by globalization and the growing number of entrepreneurs entering the international market. As a result of mergers and acquisitions, more and more companies are faced with situations in which employees are exposed to events involving "unfamiliar" colleagues at a growing speed.

It is important to keep in mind, however, that cultural tensions are not limited to people from different countries. They play a role whenever people come into contact with each other. This phenomenon can even be observed within families: half of the children in big cities in the Netherlands have at least one parent with a non-Dutch nationality. Tensions are part and parcel of family relations. Families who *do* have the same nationality can also experience large differences. Examples abound of conflict arising in stepfamilies when a new partner enters the home, bringing with them new ways of doing things that can create resistance.

The same principle applies to companies. In some cases, the culture differences exhibit themselves in the form of the sometimes-conflicting interests of various departments: the production, sales, finance, and marketing departments, for example. These divergent interests can lead to a plethora of problems, from suspicion and a bad working atmosphere to an increase of absences due to illness and large margins of error in production. As you can see, differences can have far-reaching effects.

A Tool for Dealing with Culture Differences

This book aims to give you a better grasp of more effective ways to deal with culture differences, specifically within the cadre of servant-leadership. Servant-leadership is the brainchild of the American expert in leadership in organizations Robert K. Greenleaf. It is a style of leadership that is based on the idea that leading and serving are two sides of the same coin. This is in many ways an unusual concept. For most people, leadership is connected with power, and serving is viewed as the absence thereof. In the dominating leadership models, the leader is the person who gives the orders and the "servant" is the one who takes them. In that sense, the term "leading" has a positive connotation—exactly the opposite connotation of "serving."

Servant-Leadership

Servant-leadership is totally different. This model revolves around the creation of a whole through the integration of opposites, much like the symbol of yin-yang. The secret of the servant-leader lies in the hyphen between "servant" and "leader." The hyphen represents the essence. Not only does it represent a close connection between the two concepts, but also that, in terms of content, they are fundamentally equally valued. Without that integration, *servant* would be nothing more than an adjective for *leadership*. That would make servant-leadership just another variation of the many ways you can approach leadership. Just as the word *adjective* signifies, an adjective is adjacent to the noun; it is a modifier with a different core meaning from the word it is modifying. In the case of servant-leadership, that would be completely wrong. Instead of *servant*'s being a modifier of the main word, *leadership*, servant-leader has a core meaning in itself. Together the words form a completely new compound noun, with both words making up an integral part of the same noun.

The fundamental equality of the two words has significant consequences. This is a departure from linear logic or one-way traffic of thought. Leadership can start with a desire to serve others, but it can just as easily be the other way around: the leading servant.

Simplicity

There is one more point to be made about the intersection of servant-leadership; namely, it is not complicated. Its strength, in fact, stems from the simplicity of the concept. The distinctiveness of this concept is not in the form, but rather in the content. A servant-leader combines two ideas within him- or herself that, conceptually, lie miles apart. The result: an extremely unique combination—and not only unique but also extremely strong. People set the concepts of serving and leading into motion as a result of a deep inner *drive*. Servant-leadership is a question of inner motivation, of a deeply felt mission, and everyone can become a servant-leader, regardless of where the person is, because the combination of opposites lies within everyone's reach. It gives perspective to anyone who is wrestling with the problem of cultural differences, no matter what level he or she occupies within an organization.

What applies to the concept of servant-leadership is also applicable to cultural differences: it is possible to combine opposing values. The servant-leader excels at this because he or she is used to build a bridge between two differing opinions, points of view, concepts, etc. This lessens the "us versus them" way of thinking. From a servant-leader's point of view, there is no "us" or "them"—only "we" and a common purpose.

Servant-leadership is based on the idea that, beneath all cultural differences, there is a common basis, namely, being human. On a fundamental level, we have more in common than not—including the dilemmas we have in life. We define a dilemma as a situation where one must choose between two options that seem to be in conflict with each other. This belief leads to the insight that all dilemmas in all cultures are the same, and that the only difference is the starting point and path that we each take to resolve them.

For this reason, servant-leaders are not tempted into making a choice between two opposite values, and they also avoid choosing an unsatisfactory compromise. The mark of a servant-leader is that he or she chooses a solution where both opposing value sets are combined in such a way that they are actually strengthened, not weakened. The implementation of a servant-leader in an intercultural context is a dialectical process; through thesis and antithesis, the servant-leader achieves a synthesis, which is always enriching.

The first part of this book is an introduction to servant-leadership. The theory and background of this leadership style will be laid out, as well as the influence that corporate culture has and the results that culture clashes can bring. We will then zoom in on the ability of a servant-leader to combine opposing values, as well as explaining what core qualities are necessary in order to do so.

Of course, the most important thing is what you as an entrepreneur can do to use these theories in practice. To help illustrate this, we give several concrete examples in the second part of the book. The clashes that result from cultural differences can be divided into several main categories. On the basis of our experience, we have divided the "battlefield" into seven dilemmas. Each dilemma can, in turn, be sub-divided into other dilemmas, variations on the main theme. The dilemmas clearly illustrate situations in which people in an intercultural context run into problems in practice. However, problems unto themselves are not very interesting; what is really important are the solutions. That is why we look mainly at the manner in which servant-leaders deal with these dilemmas and the way in which they combine the opposing poles, thereby strengthening them, in order to find the best possible solution.

We have noticed several things about this process. First, we have observed the universal character of the dilemmas. Precisely because both sides of the dilemma have positive aspects, people in every culture vacillate between both extremes. The *differences* between cultures exhibit themselves in the ways in which the dilemmas are approached. The second thing that became apparent was the effectiveness of the steps taken. Third, we observed large diversity in approaches and, fourth, the presence of a red thread through the various solutions. All of these points are easily explained. Servant-leadership is so effective in dealing with culture differences because of its cross-border character. It is not a dogma or a blueprint—exactly the opposite. It is a classic example of "out-of-the-box" thinking. Every culture, organization, or department can apply the concept in its own way. That also explains diversity, while the common thread is the core commitment to being of service and to mutual trust. The freedom, the result of servant-leadership, is what makes this method perfect for fulfilling its function as a bridge.

A nice theory? Indeed it is, but it is much more than just that. Servant-leadership has been applied successfully in various companies all over the world. With all of their diversity, these companies have one thing in common: they are better because of it.

Whoever puts servant-leadership into practice will notice that things change for the better and that problems, which seemed unresolvable, can actually be solved. These problems, on closer inspection, are actually not problems at all, but, instead, they are chances—the chance to use diversity to your advantage. That is why the third part of this text is a practical model, presented in a way that provides insights into your own organization.

PART I

Servant-Leadership: In a Nutshell

A UNIVERSAL GIVEN

In 1970, the American organizational expert Robert K. Greenleaf coined the term *servant-leadership* in his essay "The Servant as Leader."[1] This visionary publication brought on a new movement in the area of management.

At first glance, a servant-leader is a contradiction in terms. Someone is either a leader *or* a servant. To have both together at the same time does not seem logical. However, Robert Greenleaf merged these two seemingly opposite concepts into a practical, powerful combination. According to him, servant-leadership is a management style in which leading and serving are in harmony, and there is thoughtful interaction with the environment. A servant-leader is someone who has a strong wish to serve as well as a strong ability to lead and, most importantly, is able to combine both in such a way that they strengthen each other positively.

Background in Consulting

Greenleaf developed his vision of leadership during the many years that he worked at the telecom giant AT&T. He stood out as a management consultant because he had an unusual approach. In contrast to many of his colleagues, he not only looked at numbers and systems but also viewed these things in their context. In his early writings, he promoted the idea that "work exists for the person, as much as the person exists for the work." He was part of the avant-garde in advocating courses in listening, and he brought in theologians and philosophers for management advice. Shortly before retirement, he became a professor at the Sloan School of Management of MIT and at Harvard Business School. He also gave lectures at Dartmouth College and the University of Virginia.

Theoretical Foundation

During his work as a consultant, he was known for the idea that the purpose of leaders was to serve their people and to bring the best out of them. After he left AT&T, he began to further develop his thoughts, which led to the publication in 1970 of the essay mentioned above: *The Servant as Leader.* In various books and articles, he saw the solid foundation and possibilities for a future movement of servant-leadership. The essence of leadership is the service of others, according to Greenleaf. Servant-leadership is more than just another variation of leadership styles. It is a lifestyle that arises from the deep belief that the heart of your mission as a leader is to continually challenge others, to encourage them, and to give them a chance to develop their talents. One can spot a servant-leader, therefore, by the fact that the people around him or her also grow.

At that time, during a period in management theory that was known for hierarchy and striving for power, this was a revolutionary thought. But it was exactly that revolutionary element that appealed to people. His concept was inspiring, and people everywhere started employing it in practice. Companies that were built on this foundation often turned out to be especially successful, owing to the fact that people there were valued for their talents, which in turn resulted in highly motivated employees, better production metrics, fewer absences due to illness, and higher profits.

A Long Tradition

Though Greenleaf might have introduced the term *servant-leadership*, the idea has been around for thousands of years. Servant-leadership stems from many long and respectable traditions. Kent Keith, CEO of the Greenleaf Center for Servant-Leadership, and someone highly inspired by Robert Greenleaf, gave the following overview in his book *The Case for Servant Leadership*.[2]

Religious Belief Systems

In the Western tradition, Jesus is the epitome of a servant-leader. With his pronouncement: "I did not come to be served, but to serve," he made servitude a central principle of Christianity. John Wesley, the well-known preacher, said it more simply: "Do all the good you can, to all the people you can, for as long as you can."

The Jewish Talmud says: "All men are responsible for one another."

The Sufi sheikh M. R. Bawa Muhaiyaddeen preached: "To realize the pain and suffering of others, and to offer your hands in assistance, to help alleviate their suffering, that is Islam."

The classic Tao scripture, Tao Te Ching, reads: "The way to heaven is to benefit others and to not injure."

The Hindu Bhagavad Gita states: "Through selfless service, you will always be fruitful and find the fulfillment of your desires. That is the promise of the Creator . . . he is present in every act of service."

And finally, the Buddhist text Shantideva, or the Path of the Bodhisattva: "If I employ others for my own purposes, I myself shall experience servitude. But if I use myself for the sake of others, I shall experience only lordliness."

The Ancients

Plato can be seen as one of the authors of this principle. He named four virtues for the basis of a good life: courage, righteousness, moderation, and wisdom—the pillars of servant-leadership.

Aristotle answered the question of what is the essence of life: "To serve others and do good."

And the Roman orator and philosopher Cicero said: "Men were brought into existence for the sake of men that they might do one another good."

The Modern Age

This idea is also visible in the modern age. For example, Albert Schweitzer said, "The purpose of human life is to serve and to show compassion and the will to help others."

Martin Luther King Jr. said the same thing in a different way: "Life's most persistent question is: What are you doing for others?"

The Indian poet Rabindranath Tagore was more poetic when he philosophized, "I awoke and saw that life is service. I acted and, behold, service was joy."

One of the most well-known servant-leaders of the twentieth century was Mother Teresa, who was quoted as saying, "There is joy in transcending yourself to serve others."

The importance of service is clearly a universal given—and that says something about the value of this principle. Universal values are actually an expression of wisdom.

Current Management Thinking

Today's management gurus also have positive things to say about servant-leadership. Many have been influenced by Robert Greenleaf. In his book *The Fifth Discipline*,[3] Peter Senge is quoted as saying: "In the past thirty years, no one has had a more profound effect on Leadership thought than Robert Greenleaf." Warren Bennis, author of *On Becoming a Leader*,[4] has the opinion: "When dealing with leadership, I believe that Greenleaf and his writings are the most original, useful, accessible, and moral."

Ken Blanchard, author of *Leading at a Higher Level*,[5] writes:

> *I sincerely believe that servant-leadership has never been as applicable in the world of leadership as it is today. People are looking not only for a higher goal, for meaning and for ways to rise to the challenges of a changing world; but also for the principles and views that really work. Servant-leadership works. Servant-leadership teaches you how you can bring people to a higher level by leading them there.*

In Jim Collins's article "Level 5 Leadership," he describes the "level 5 leader" as someone with a special mix between professional willpower and personal modesty. [6] This is also another reference to servant-leadership.

Stephen Covey, author of *The Seven Habits of Highly Effective People*,[7] is also in favor of servant-leadership. He says: "At the core of our being there is the thing we draw upon to rise above our current circumstances and our nature. When you do this, you can tap into an entirely new source of human motivation." That is exactly why Robert Greenleaf's servant-leadership ideas are so stirring, encouraging, and inspirational.

There are important changes taking place in the world, changes that stem from two forces. The first is the dramatic rate of globalization of both markets and technology. This change strengthens the impact of the second: timeless, universal principles that are the foundation for every kind of lasting success.

One of these fundamental, timeless principles is the idea of servant-leadership. We are convinced that its importance will grow even more. People are under continual pressures to produce more for less money, and in less time than ever before. The only way that this will be achieved is through *empowerment,* giving people the necessary tools. And the only way to achieve that is to create a culture of trust, where bosses are transformed into servants and coaches. That is precisely what servant-leadership stands for.

Leaders are starting to learn that this kind of *empowerment* is the most important. For organizations, it is this principle that makes the difference between sustained success and their possible downfall.

Self-Realization

"A servant-leader loves people, and wants to help them. The mission of the servant-leader is therefore to identify the needs of others," says Kent Keith.[8]

That is exactly what makes servant-leadership so effective and why, according to Keith, it is so much more than yet another leadership model. According to him, servant-leadership is nothing less than "the creation of a better world":

> *I have no doubt that the world will be a better place when more leaders and organizations practice servant leadership. I also have no doubt that servant leadership is best for the leader. It is the most meaningful, satisfying way to lead. It is not about self-denial or self-sacrifice. It is about* self-fulfillment.

What appeals to him most in terms of servant-leadership is the readiness and capability to reconcile opposites and to optimize on diversity. In 1968, in the middle of student protests the world over, Kent Keith published a booklet for student leaders that included "The Paradoxical Commandments."[9] He wanted to support his fellow students by showing them that it was possible to get things done, even with polar opposites.

The Paradoxical Commandments of Leadership

- People are illogical, unreasonable, and self-centered. Love them anyway.
- If you do good, people will accuse you of selfish ulterior motives. Do good anyway.

- If you are successful, you will win false friends and true enemies.
  Succeed anyway.
- The good you do today will be forgotten tomorrow.
  Do good anyway.
- Honesty and frankness make you vulnerable.
  Be honest and frank anyway.
- The biggest men and women with the biggest ideas can be shot down by the smallest men and women with the smallest minds.
  Think big anyway.
- People favor underdogs but follow only top dogs.
  Fight for a few underdogs anyway.
- What you spend years building may be destroyed overnight.
  Build anyway.
- People really need help but may attack you if you do help them.
  Help people anyway.
- Give the world the best you have and you'll get kicked in the teeth.
  Give the world the best you have anyway.

Lasting Solutions

The "paradoxical commandments" describe perfectly what servant-leadership is all about. The message is clear: even in the most difficult situations, it is possible to find an alternative. How? According to Keith, the answer is: by confronting the worst in the world with the best in ourselves. In the end, it is not the circumstances that determine how the world looks; it is *our reactions*—and these reactions can always be positive!

Herein lies the key to resolving dilemmas, no matter what kind they are. The paradoxical commandments are custom-made for servant-leaders because they focus on personal meaning. Instead of letting themselves be led by their circumstances, servant-leaders are internally driven, starting from within themselves and guided by their own morals. As a result, they are not thrown off by problems and they are not dependent on recognition. Whereas the classic *power* model gets stuck in problems, a servant-leader's internal compass provides the possibility of lasting solutions.

Notes

1   Robert K. Greenleaf, *The Servant as Leader*, first distributed as pamphlet in 1970 [revised edition] (Indianapolis, IN: Robert K. Greenleaf Center, 1991).

2   Kent M. Keith, *The Case for Servant Leadership* (Westfield, IN: Greenleaf Center for Servant-Leadership, 2008).

3   Peter M. Senge, *The Fifth Discipline: The Art and Practice of the Learning Organization* (London: Random House Business Books; 2nd revised edition, 2006).

4   Warren Bennis, *On Becoming a Leader* (New York City: Basic Books; revised edition, 2003).

5   Ken Blanchard, "Foreword: The Heart of Servant Leadership," in Larry C. Spears and Michele Lawrence, eds., *Focus on Leadership* (New York: John Wiley & Sons, Inc., 2001), xi.

6   Jim Collins, "Level 5 Leadership: The Triumph of Humility and Fierce Resolve," in *Best of Harvard Business Review*, HBR, July–August, 2005.

7   Stephen Covey, "Foreword: Servant Leadership from the Inside out," in Larry C. Spears, ed., *Insights on Leadership* (New York: John Wiley & Sons, Inc., 1998), xi–xii.

8   Kent M. Keith, *The Case for Servant Leadership* (Westfield, IN: Greenleaf Center for Servant-Leadership, 2008).

9   Kent M. Keith, *The Silent Revolution: Dynamic Leadership in the Student Council* (Cambridge, MA: Harvard Student Agencies, 1968). The author's explanation of the paradoxical commandments can be found in *Anyway: The Paradoxical Commandments* (New York: G. P. Putnam's Sons, 2002).

FROM A *POWER*
TO A *SERVICE* MODEL

The world is changing at top speed. This is also true about work relationships, which in turn has consequences for views of leadership. The dominant leadership model—the *power* model—is fizzling out. There is a cry for a serious alternative.[1]

When talking about leadership, most companies use the power model. According to this model, leadership is all about the attainment, exercise, and retention of power. The boss has only one goal: to ensure that people do what he or she wants. It consists mostly of handy strategies to win. Ethics and morals do not come into the vocabulary or, at best, do so only as an afterthought.

The problem with the power model is that power has become a goal in and unto itself and that the attainment of power depends on choosing one or another opposite. In this model, power is a scarce good and invites competition. The person that finally has it needs to defend it tooth and nail. Sharing is completely out of the question. This results in conflicts between various groups and factions. The idea that leadership is about beating the other group sits deep in old management ideology. This is a shame because internal fighting is a waste of precious energy; rivalry and infighting are not productive. The ambition for power also shades one's view of success. Success is then defined in terms of power, rather than what you have achieved for the organization or for the community. In addition to that, power is addictive. You can never get enough and as a result it can have a corrupting effect.

Double Focus

Thus a need for a leadership model with a more productive approach: the wish to serve others. In large part, this model is referred to as "servant-leadership" because of the motive. Power is not seen as irrelevant, but consciously used in order to serve. People working within this model are called servant-leaders.

Companies that implement servant-leadership are very successful as a result. How is it that servant-leadership succeeds where the unilateral power model fails in combining opposites? The answer can be found in the double focus of a servant-leader. The power model tilts heavily in favor of leading and is out of balance, whereas servant-leadership integrates both serving *and* leading, or, even better, serving *by* leading or leading *by* serving. This is a much broader basis that results in a more harmonious management style.

A servant-leader knows that his or her own growth comes from facilitating the growth of others, who are the final deliverers of the output. In addition, this double focus fits perfectly with the raison d'être of the company. Companies derive their existence from what they can do for the community. Whether discussing private, public, government, or nonprofit companies, the ultimate goal is to be forthcoming in meeting the needs of humankind. Regardless of whether the people are clients, patients, students, or citizens, if things are going well, they are core. At the bottom of it all, every company has a serving function. In practice, however, that realization is rarely made. All too often, entrepreneurs are at the center of their own world and the universal value of service has been replaced with shareholder value. As a result, corporations have in some cases become isolated from the community and cut off from their own roots.

Back to Basics

Servant-leadership is actually a reaction. This leadership style consciously goes *back to basics*. That means more than is maybe apparent at first appearance. In this model, leaders are not triggered by the search for money and power, but rather by the question: "What do people need and what can I do to make sure they get it?" In that light, the most important job for leaders is to find out what the needs of the community are and to fulfill them. In some ways, you can say that the power model is all about taking, while the service model is about giving, which is a completely different paradigm.

Working with this paradigm is only possible when people are both capable and motivated, however. Therefore, in addition to making sure the wishes of clients are satisfied, it is important to pay attention to the needs of your employees. It is important to understand that work is about more than just earning money—especially these days. People are looking for meaning in their work, and they can only find this if they are given the chance to use their talents. And that is precisely what servant-leaders do: they serve their employees and, in the process, they serve their clients as well. In the bigger view, they are also serving the world, the shareholders, and themselves. A path that one can also take in the opposite direction, and where there are different starting points.

Alternatives

There are many different ways to deal with culture differences. Within the power model, the leader usually follows his or her own path without looking back. The other extreme is also possible: *When in Rome, do as the Romans do*. The latter is good in terms of being accepted by others in unfamiliar situations, but your own authenticity is lost in the process. In addition to that, the "Romans" would see your behavior as that of a second-rate actor.

There is also the more "adult" alternative: the compromise. This seems to be the best solution by far. When you both want something else, you cannot both get what you want, so you both sacrifice something to a certain extent. In this way, you get a bit of what you wanted in the first place, and so does the other. Therefore, you will both be happy, right?

Well, in any case, neither of you will be *completely* satisfied because the sign of a compromise is that you meet each other halfway. This means that both parties have to give something up. The result is often presented as the best possible solution considering the options and, therefore, a win-win situation. In reality, however, it is a disguised loss.

Connecting

The service model, on the other hand, answers the problems by overcoming the opposites. While the power model follows the principle of divide and rule, the service model is defined by reconciliation. The idea that opposites exist to be combined, because that is the way in which you can best serve people, is a novel thought. That is why servant-leaders look not at what separates people, but rather at what brings them together. According to servant-leaders, culture differences are not problems; they are chances—opportunities to create something together that is stronger than the two parts. Instead of watering down your own point of view, you can enjoin the opposite to make it watertight, turning your disadvantages into an advantage for both.

Unity

This entire process can only occur when there is an atmosphere of mutual trust. This trust comes out of the understanding that, at the deepest level, there is a commonality that all people share. Differences are a certainty, but it is better not to increase them unnecessarily. It is an art to bring out those things that unify, with an open mind and respect for cultural differences. Beneath every difference, there is a shared foundation: humanity. There is recognition at the deepest levels because, all over the planet, people have the same big questions: What is the purpose of life? How can I be happy? What is my purpose on this earth? The answers that people come up with in different cultures are determined historically and culturally. With this view, we are suddenly no longer dealing with insurmountable differences, but with different accents. This realization is a productive basis for intercultural management, a solid foundation that can be built upon. When people have this frame of reference, reconciliation is within reach.

It was this kind of thinking that drove the merger of the Dutch temp agencies Randstad and Vedior in 2008. During the integration they did *not* hire an expensive consulting company to come in and iron out the culture differences, but instead organized "get-togethers" where the employees were able to meet and get to know each other simply as people. Instead of focusing on the large differences between the two organizations and finding tools to deal with the differences, people across the organization were zooming in on the underlying foundation. At every level and in every department, employees were invited to share their personal stories with their new colleagues. Meeting others for the first time via *emotional lifelines,* during which people shared the important moments in their lives with each other, including past mistakes and painful memories, created a strong bond. "People are people, regardless of their cultural background," explained Tex Gunning, then CEO of Vedior and a believer in an interpersonal approach. "Focusing on what you share and the ways in which you resemble each other leads to a sense of connection, humanity, and compassion. If you come together at the most fundamental levels, you will see each other eye-to-eye. That makes sustainable change possible."[2]

Notes

1   The authors are indebted to Kent M. Keith for ideas shared in this chapter. See Kent M. Keith, *The Case for Servant Leadership* (Westfield, IN: Greenleaf Center for Servant-Leadership, 2008), Chapter 3, "Power Model vs. Service Model."
2   Personal interview, 2007.

CULTURE CLASHES

3

The ultimate test of a model is in applying it to those situations that seem to be irresolvable. Often this is the case in situations of tremendous diversity, making culture clashes one of the larger challenges facing management.

Fear of the unknown is completely natural. Each person is at the center of his or her own world and sees things from a unique perspective. He or she determines what is normal. When another person does something unexpected, this leads to discomfort because you do not understand the other person's logic, you feel shut out, or you feel 100 percent confident that your way of doing things is the best. Value judgments are almost automatic when dealing with culture differences. Fear of a foreign culture arises from the idea that the unknown value systems deny those that you believe in and value. This puts everything that is precious to you in danger. Fear can lead to distrust, negativity, and the tendency to fight, tooth and nail, for your own opinions. This tendency is unproductive and can even be extremely destructive.

You can look at it in another way. Instead of focusing on differences, you can look instead at the similarities, because these are undeniable. As John F. Kennedy said:

> In the final analysis, our most basic common link is that we all inhabit this small planet. We all breathe the same air. We all cherish our children's futures, and we are all mortal. [1]

In that light, culture differences melt like snow in the burning sun.

Misunderstandings

The problem is that differences never *really* lessen. They are still there—you just pretend not to see them. That is a bit less damaging than the first point of view, but cultural relativism does not do justice to the colorful reality in which people from different walks of life can live and work together, with all the visible and invisible obstacles that result.

The reality is that cooperating with people who, literally and figuratively, speak different languages can be quite a task. This is true not only for cultures that are very far apart in terms of values and ideas, but also for cultures that are seemingly very similar. It is relatively easier to prepare the direct and transparent Dutchman for a trip to subtle, indirect Japan than to get him ready for a trip to Antwerp. In the latter case, you often hear, "No problem; we speak the same language." It is exactly this kind of underestimation of the differences that has caused so many problems in Belgian-Dutch communications. In many ways, the Belgians are even less transparent than the Japanese. At the other extreme, American-French interactions have also often been doomed to failure because of the desire on both sides to try to control their environment. There is nothing wrong with this approach, but when you put these two together, it can sometimes lead to disaster!

Deciding Factor

Obviously cultural differences have an impact, and they need to be taken seriously. The influence of culture should not be underestimated. It is one factor that influences every single other process within an organization. You can compare it to what "water" means to a swimmer: it is the most basic element, the context in which it all happens. As a professional, you can do everything within your power in terms of training and skills in order to win the world championship, but all that is worthless if it is not in keeping with the environment in which the event takes place. Techniques that work in still waters may not necessarily also work in water with a current. This is because, although water seems to be neutral, it is not. It penetrates everything and encloses the swimmer on all sides and is thus a deciding factor in success or failure.

This is also the case with culture. Whether we are talking about finance, logistics, or production, culture influences all of it. The integration of two organizations, or two departments, with different cultural backgrounds requires an active role on the part of management. An effective approach starts with identifying the frames of reference within which people are operating. Clashes on the work floor are almost always a result of value differences; therefore, it is important to carefully get a handle on what those values are. In general, problems can be categorized under one of the following seven dilemmas:

1. leading-serving
2. rules-exceptions
3. parts-the whole
4. control-passion
5. specific-diffuse
6. short term–long term
7. push-pull

In the second part of the book we will discuss these in further detail.

Dilemmas

These dilemmas give rise to many questions. Are leaders responsible for setting standards and making and communicating rules, or are they to orchestrate the necessary exceptions to the rule? Are they abstract thinkers at a higher level, or are they masters of detail? Can a leader also be a servant? These, and similar questions, lead to the most important question of our time: are leaders people who are brought in by shareholders in order to maximize their profit, or are leaders the people who are responsible for developing others and adding something to the community at large?

These kinds of question make it clear that there are an infinite number of ways to define good leadership. Read Warren Bennis and you get the impression that leadership is all about vision, mission, and transparency. Read French literature and you discover that the most famous leaders are a product of their education. Whereas, the Japanese idea of a good leader is: a man, a senior, and an alumnus of the University of Tokyo!

Challenges

The diversity in points of view poses a challenge for corporate life, especially because modern man is very demanding. For example, we want an extremely fast computer that is *also* user-friendly; we want to be protected from terrorism *without* this protection's invading our privacy; and we want a fast car that is *also* safe. We want it all. This is true whether we are talking about products and services or processes. Even different departments in the same company, such as research and development, marketing, and after-sales, have their own, often conflicting, interests. Conventional wisdom says that, in this case, we must choose. But is that really necessary?

Systematic Analysis

Over the years, the authors of this book have looked at the intercultural world behind the scenes in hundreds of companies and have judged the effectiveness of the most widespread leadership styles. Interviews with various business leaders have been systematically analyzed and run through the scientific gauntlet. This has resulted in important insights about the best ways to deal with cultural differences. In this process it is imperative to realize that one standpoint is not better than another; both extremes have advantages and disadvantages, and both are disastrous when taken too far.

One thing is very clear: the success of various companies is more and more dependent on their ability to bridge cultural differences. It appears that, in an intercultural environment, the most important competence for leaders is the ability to integrate apparently opposite values. That is certainly not easy, but it is possible. Take Formula One, for example. This perfectly illustrates how a fast car can also be safe, but the cars had to be designed with a completely new approach.

Circles

In other words, the viewpoint that opposing values are the two extremes on opposite sides of a linear scale needs to be thrown out of the window. What is impossible in linear logic, per definition—combining two opposites—is possible in cyclical logic. The servant-leader bends, as it were, the two extremes toward each other, which results in the line's becoming a circle, a circle that no longer has opposing values. Everything is connected in cyclical logic and flows from one part to another in an organic way. There is no "first" or "last" because there is no set path from A to B. Perhaps you do not want to go from A to B, but from B to A! That is also possible because a circle is two-directional, which means that what were originally opposing values now flow naturally from one to the other, strengthening both.

Solutions

When you use cyclical thought to deal with the dilemmas that occur in every organization, there is room for solutions. These solutions can start at any point in the circle, and the best part is that it also *happens*. All around the world, companies are wrestling with the same dilemmas, but the paths they choose to resolve them are as different as night and day. The different ways depend entirely on the cultural background of the people. Every servant-leader has his or her own starting point, a starting point that is determined by personal culture, personal organization, and personal temperament.

As a result, people from totally different starting points, and via different paths, can still come to the same solutions. What these solutions have in common, and how you can identify them, is that they are harmonious, they are efficient, and they can count on wide support. The ability to overcome linear thinking and structurally reconcile cultural dilemmas is referred to here as *cross-cultural competence*.

To sum it up—servant-leadership is fundamentally different in that it moves us:

- *From linear to cyclical thinking*
- *From one-way to two-way direction*
- *From choosing between two opposite values to combining them*
- *From one-dimensional to holistic*
- *From top-down to bottom-up*
- *From analysis to synthesis*

Practice

The servant-leadership approach of integrating opposites that is recommended here is anything but "out-there." The belief that the key to resolving problems can be found by combining opposing values is based on thousands of real-life stories, shared by entrepreneurs all over the world. At the consulting company Trompenaars Hampden-Turner (THT) these experiences have been scientifically documented for many years, creating a treasure trove of information. As a result, which approach works with which problems is something that has been explored in detail. If one thing has become clear, it is that when it comes to intercultural dilemmas, there is no standard approach. On the other hand, there is one constant in endless diversity: the approach of combining opposites *works*. THT's database, which holds the culture values of 90,000 people, with 8,000 dilemmas validated with 1,500 interviews, supports this.

Another source is the servant-leadership movement. The Greenleaf Center for Servant-Leadership in America, and the center in Europe by the same name, offer a wealth of experience when it comes to organizations that work with servant-leadership. It is often said that of the top ten companies listed in *Fortune*'s *100 Best Companies to Work For in America,* six are based on the principles of servant-leadership, including TDIndustries, Synovis, the coffee chain Starbucks, and Southwest Airlines.[2]

Notes

1   John F. Kennedy, speech at The American University, Washington, DC, June 10, 1963.
2   *Fortune*'s *100 Best Companies to Work For in America* (http://money.cnn.com/magazines/fortune/bestcompanies/2008/index.html).

CORE QUALITIES 4

What is the secret of servant-leadership? That question is not an easy one to answer. One of the most noticeable things about this leadership style is the absence of "the best way." There are numerous ways to achieve the desired goal. Your *attitude* when approaching someone is most important in determining the progress, and the solution, of possible points at issue.

Diversity and flexibility are important concepts of servant-leadership. With all of their differences, servant-leaders have several things in common. Their starting point is always the same: the readiness to serve others. That is what resonates through all of their actions. In order to make that happen, servant-leaders bring people with different points of view together and know how to transform the resulting tension into a productive dynamic. The leader is not soft, but actually hard in that the leader is explicit about the core values, including respect for diversity.

Servant-leadership literature is full of advice and characteristics of these leaders. Most notably, it is mostly written from a Western perspective. An Eastern perspective, in contrast, tells you that a leader needs to listen instead of talk, act from the bottom up instead of top down, and work as part of a community instead of putting focus only on individuals. The point we are making is not that a leader has to trade one of these values in for another, but that he or she knows how to use both most effectively. The servant-leaders can be better speakers if they know how to listen, can use their power more effectively if they know how to let it go, and can build teams of creative individuals. In other words, the most important quality of a servant-leader is that he or she can reunite opposites. This is true on many levels. In the light of intercultural management, seven core qualities have been formulated.

1 Leading Through Serving

This basic principle makes it clear that both serving and leading are two important qualities that often conflict. The term *servant-leadership* shows that the two can be reconciled. By serving, you become a strong leader, and the strength of your leadership is determined by the extent to which you give others room to grow in their own lives during the period in which they work for your company. Every parent knows what this means. On the one hand, you teach your children to follow the family rules; on the other hand, you want to nurture them as individuals to develop and grow. In the corporate world, however, combining both aspects is often forgotten. A servant-leader, though, does this and thereby knows how to empower his or her employees.

Leading Oneself

Opportunity and responsibility go hand in hand. They are two sides of the same coin. Servant-leadership proposes that everyone is his or her own leader. That means that everyone in a family, organization, department, or community is the pinnacle of his or her own pyramid. It is within everyone's reach to find out and fulfill the needs of others. This has far-reaching consequences, and it is especially important in situations where there is polarization, because the basis of "us" versus "them" thinking thereby falls by the wayside.

In every company, people complain: department about department, white collar about blue collar, production about sales and vice versa. And all too often, the complaint is that management has no idea as to what is actually going on. Everyone is busy with personal ambitions, position, power, and search for opportunity. Employees frequently have the feeling that they are not involved in the decision-making process. "They just do what they want," is the oft-heard criticism.

In companies where servant-leadership is practiced, however, you cannot get away with this criticism; the reason being that leadership comes with responsibility. If you are dissatisfied with the way things are going, then you should not just carry on without doing something about it. That will not bring you any closer to your goal. A better alternative is to take responsibility and chart the problem in such a way that you can see both sides. You need to take your responsibilities and address them such that the dichotomy can be resolved. In this manner, all people are responsible for the world around them. This is equally true at work as in private life.

Turning the Pyramid on Its Head

The traditional pyramid with the CEO at the top and an extensive army of "the little people" at the base is not effective. In that kind of structure, people worry more about what the boss wants, or does not want, than what the client wants. This asks for unorthodox measures. In order to change the way we look, it is necessary to turn the pyramid upside down.

Another problem with the traditional pyramid is that necessary information often does not filter up to the top. People have a tendency to say what they think the management team would like to hear, instead of what management needs to hear. The problems can be tackled by ascribing leadership a different status, one of first among equals. By making CEOs part of the team, leadership transforms from an individual responsibility to a shared responsibility, which gives rise to a better connection between the organization and the client.

Finally, the servant-leader is in the position to reverse the pyramid whenever that is necessary. It is more important to be able to rotate the pyramid than just turning it upside down.

Empowerment

When people have enough room to develop themselves and are given responsibility, they are able to reach their full potential. This releases all kinds of mental energy and motivation, which ensures that people are at their best. This process is referred to as *empowerment*. Every person has certain talents. The big question is not only whether people have enough room, but also whether they actually have the chance to grow. In many companies, there are people working beneath their level. They are only expected to do the tasks that they were hired to do. Other talents that they have are unused. That is a real shame.

A servant-leader first looks at someone's potential and then tries to match that potential within that person's field of work. Development is not reserved only for management. At every level, in every position, people have to take the opportunity to bring the best out of themselves, because the best for themselves is also the best for the company and, in the broader perspective, for the world at large.

2 Better Rules Through Exceptions

Servant-leaders do not care for the choice between rules and exceptions; they ask instead how each strengthens the other, resulting in better rules. Good rules are strong enough to allow exceptions. This insight deals with the dilemma between a *rule-based* approach and a *principle-based* approach. It is impossible to have totalitarian rules in the world, as the *rule-based* point of view strives for. The beautiful thing about a *principle-based* approach is that rules are present in principles, while rules do not carry principles within them.

The servant-leader is extremely good at building a bridge between a *rule-based* (rule- and text-driven) approach and a *principle-based* (exception- and context-driven) approach. The power is in the combination, like *mass-customization*, which is a result of Henry Ford's *mass production* and the Japanese-developed *customization*.

Henry Ford was a servant-leader because he asked the question: "Do my clients want faster horses or an alternative form of transportation?" The question arose from the desire to be of service, which resulted in a solution that was better than anything they could think of themselves. Herein lies the core and power of servant-leadership.

Mistakes as a Way to Improve

An important sign of servant-leadership is the view that the mistakes people make are actually chances for improvement. Leadership is only effective if you have a continually improving system by which people can learn from unusual mistakes. An individual or company that never makes mistakes cannot also make progress. The servant-leader will always try to see the mistakes that others make as opportunities to learn and grow further. The strongest countries, organizations, and individuals are continually learning from *best practices.*

3 Building Teams of Creative Individuals

Here again, the servant-leader is able to reconcile the important parts of the two extremes. It is a core quality of a servant-leader to be able to use the creativity of individuals for the better performance of the team. On the other side, the team shall do everything possible to increase the creativity of the individual.

Community Building

This positive way of dealing with people has greater implications for the atmosphere within a company. There is a transformation from a mere gathering of individuals to a team in which everyone uses personal talents to contribute to a shared goal. Through community building, a company changes from just a place to earn money into a community, *a place you want to be*—somewhere where people treat each other well, take responsibility for each other, and, with a sense of involvement, work toward a shared mission. In such a group, differences are surmountable. Looking for factors that connect and stimulate a feeling of belonging is of great importance for such a company. Power stems from the fact that the whole is many times more than the sum of its parts.

4 More Passion as a Result of Control

In his description of "level 5 leaders," Jim Collins mentions that sometimes servant-leaders seem boring and less colorful than, and in stark contrast to, "level 3 managers," for example, who are more expressive and come across as having a big ego. These level 3 managers express their authority. Servant-leaders do have passion. They just know how to show their emotions at the right moments, in the context of controlled humility. They are absolutely not cold, emotionless beings.

Humor

One of the ways in which a servant-leader can bring feeling into a rational process is with humor. Humor is a typical sign of a servant-leader because people tend to smile when two irreconcilable logics both appear logical. In this way, a servant-leader uses humor to discuss opposites in a team and to bring together these qualities in order to increase output. A servant-leader would never use humor at another's expense. Only a tasteful and intelligent humor can act as a bridge.

5 Putting Parts into a Whole

A servant-leader has a helicopter overview. He or she is not only capable of seeing the forest, however, but also able to zoom in on the trees. This is the way that servant-leaders can keep an eye on specific corporate goals while not losing sight of the development of their people. This is in stark contrast to the current striving for shareholder value at the cost of employee education and training. People are also inspired and motivated by the servant-leader who gives them a clear view of the organizational goals and corporate direction. In this way, the criteria for control are more specific, fewer, and of a higher quality.

Education

Servant-leadership can never be limited to top or middle management. It is something you must do at every level. The next step is, therefore, to invest in your people, as they are the most important link to the client. It is important to teach employees about the necessity of listening and serving. If people in the organization lack this core quality, none of the desired ideals can be attained. Therefore, as a company, you must be brave enough to pull out all the stops in order to increase involvement and to provide people with the skills necessary to practice servant-leadership wherever they are within the organization. That investment will produce a hundredfold return. If you take good care of your employees, they will in turn take good care of the clients.

There are companies that believe in this so strongly that they have raised the concern for their employees to the level of their company mission statement. An example of this is the previously mentioned Texan company TDIndustries, a regular on *Fortune*'s list of *100 Best Companies to Work For in America*. TDIndustries really cares about its people. It says a lot that the company's mission statement is not about profit or being the best in its industry; it is about the development of its people. It states:

> *We are committed to providing outstanding career opportunities by exceeding our customers" expectations through continuous aggressive improvement. . . . We believe in continuous, intense "people-development" efforts, including substantial training budgets.* [1]

Commitment to Growth

The best way to let people grow is via coaching and mentoring. That is nothing new. In the Middle Ages people were already using this model of master and apprentice. However, the outdated management idea that says employees need to be controlled has no place in servant-leadership. Instead of micromanagement, it is much better to focus on motivation. In situations where understanding, knowledge, and enthusiasm exist, people are excellent at fulfilling their duties, without having someone look over their shoulder. In fact, the latter is actually counterproductive. Jack Lowe Jr., chairman of TDIndustries, has this to say:

> *Your best employees have the talent and ability to leave your company and find work elsewhere if they want to. So you should lead them the way you lead volunteers.* [2]

And how do you deal with volunteers? Not by being domineering, and not through distrust or control; otherwise they will be gone in a heartbeat. To get commitment from people, you have to work on involving them and give them the chance to use their talents and contribute. Commitment to the growth of employees forms the basis of a coaching leadership style. A servant-leader can always be recognized by the fact that people around him or her are growing and developing.

Conceptualizing

A company that is built in this way has a lot of potential. Such an organization exceeds the level of single actions and sees the bigger picture. Big changes only occur as a result of big dreams and people who dare to take a different path. Only dreaming, however, is not enough. In addition to having a clear picture of what you want to achieve, you need to have the intention and the persistence to bring that dream to reality. A servant-leader is, by definition, visionary. Convinced of the fact that circumstances are not the determining factor, servant-leaders believe that it is the way you deal with circumstances that creates reality. In the end, all people create their own world with their thoughts and deeds. "Conceptualizing" means nothing more than making a connection between the desired future and the current situation, and taking the steps that are necessary to get from here to there. It is in this last step that the servant-leader joins the whole with the parts.

6 Short-Term and Long-Term Vision

A servant-leader not only is able to view things in the long term but also knows that the long term consists of several short-term decisions and results. He or she directs short-term results in the context of the long term. Servant-leaders know better than anyone that the future of an organization has more meaning when people have respect for the traditions of the past.

Looking Forward

Building a company as described here is not a piece of cake. It requires knowledge, insight, and the ability to anticipate. The ability to look forward is an absolute requirement. A servant-leader needs to foresee potential developments in order to set the right direction. This is not a case of reading tea leaves or gazing into a crystal ball. It is more about the ability to learn from mistakes *as well as* things that went well, and to build on that into the future. This means that you should not wait until problems occur, but that you anticipate them and react proactively, taking steps to prevent events from going that far. This is a question of one part logic, one part intuition.

7 Combining Internal and External

Finally, another core quality of a servant-leader is the ability to combine the internal world with the external one and vice versa. Servant-leaders are not led by the client; rather, they know that the client is counting on a surprising product or service, developed by the company out of view of the client. Pull is reunited with push. Also, with reference to the individual's internal and external worlds, it is often mentioned that servant-leaders are good listeners. This is self-explanatory, because servant-leaders are *active* listeners—passive listening does not take you as far.

Active Listening

The most important job for a servant-leader is to meet the needs of people. This is only possible if you know what these needs are. In order to make these needs clear, you have to be able to listen well. Listening is an art that few people have mastered. How many times have you been thinking about what you will say while someone else is speaking? In that case, you listen to what the other is saying only for how it relates to your own point and how you can build on what the other says in order to bring your own message across. Thus, you miss the essence of real communication. True communication begins with being open to what others have to say, giving them the room to share their complaints, wishes, and dreams. Truly listening happens only from an attitude of respect, attention, and ability to empathize. The ability to listen, to actually hear, and to converse effectively without making any value judgments is an art in itself, and one possessed by servant-leaders.

No one benefits from vacant philosophizing. A good servant-leader always keeps the goal in view, making clear what people's needs are in order to meet those needs, and moving toward that goal by asking the right questions. In addition, as a good servant-leader, you need to be open and critical of yourself and to anticipate changing situations. Times are changing, especially in terms of massive economic, demographic, and technological changes. Whoever does not change will lag behind those that do. Continuous focus needs to be placed on improvement, and active listening is the key.

Compassion

It is also extremely important that, as an entrepreneur, you are well prepared for the intercultural playing field and that you are able to put yourself in the shoes, and in the culture, of the other. It is helpful, for example, for Westerners to know that Chinese businessmen work according to the Qing-Li-Fa model. Qing stands for the heart, emotion, liking each other, the spark, and friendship. In fact, a Chinese person can only do business with someone if there is a connection. When everything on the emotional level is fine, Li comes into the picture. Now it becomes important whether or not the two companies have a logical and practical fit. If that is the case, then it is time for the third step: Fa. Fa stands for law and the rules. This model sits deeply in Chinese culture. Misunderstandings are commonplace when you, as a foreigner without this knowledge, sit at the negotiation table with a Chinese business partner. The Chinese do not understand, for example, why an American party will have a whole slew of lawyers along on the first visit. To them, that is the wrong order, as they prefer first to examine the Qing and Li aspects before arriving at Fa. To approach people in an acceptable manner for the Chinese cannot be done without empathy.

Successfulness

Listening, coaching, anticipating . . . Prominent minds in the areas of leadership and management agree that these are important elements of successful leadership. They use different names and use various formulas, but what you call it is not important. What is important is that it *works*.

Also important is the ability to connect the qualities with those that are diametrically opposite them. Combining listening with speaking, for example; or coaching and being coached; anticipating while examining the past: these are the things that make servant-leadership unique. It is also special that it does not matter where you begin. Remember, a circle never has a starting point. It is all about combining opposites to create wholeness, much like yin and yang, an integrated whole.

It is precisely this that makes this leadership philosophy so effective between cultures. Certain cultures have a preference to start from rules and then make exceptions, while other cultures would rather go from the special situations to the general principles. In some cultures, people prefer to look at the details and then place those details in the big picture, while others prefer to know the larger context first, within which the details fall. And finally, a servant-leader does not have to begin with serving. You can also begin with leading, as long as it contributes to the quality of serving! Or you can change course today!

The best part is, it is not about having impossible qualities or making expensive investments. Servant-leadership is about the attitudes and behaviors within everyone's reach and available to every organization. You can start today!

Radar and Thrust

Servant-leaders are continually working on further developing themselves, and stimulating others as well. In order to do this, there are two important orientations to consider: radar (inward) and thrust (outward).

Servant-leaders first develop their "radar" with which they advance the ability to continually feel what is important at any given moment for the further development of a person, an organization, and/or society as a whole. At the same time, they use "thrust," the ability to do that which contributes to the sustainable future of people all over the world.

The four elements of radar:

1. *Listening*
   Being open to what is said, and what is not said.
2. *Empathy*
   Recognizing people for their specific and unique personalities.
3. *Penetrating*
   Being very attentive and looking at situations from all angles.
4. *Looking forward*
   Being on top of what is coming in the future.

The four elements of thrust:

1. *Formulating a vision*
   Laying out the main lines toward the future, both inspirational and practical.
2. *Transferring*
   Stimulating people to wholeheartedly and voluntarily cooperate (though not free of obligation) in the building of a shared future.

continued ⌐

3. *Building relationships*
   Helping people to be whole, in harmony with themselves and others.
4. *Stewardship*
   Working toward a sustainable harmony between people, organizations, and society.

(Source: Greenleaf Center for Servant-Leadership Europe)

Notes

1   TDIndustries website (tdindustries.com/cultures-values.aspx).
2   Kent Keith, personal communication with Jack Lowe Jr., August 20, 2007 (Westfield, IN: Greenleaf Center for Servant-Leadership, 2008), 48.

PART II

Servant-Leadership in the Intercultural Practice

Part I dealt with the theory behind servant-leadership.

Part II is about how to use the theory in reality. As servant-leadership is the result of a combination of a unique leader and a unique team in unique circumstances, there is unfortunately no recipe for success, or template for a typical servant-leadership approach. It is possible, however, to get an idea of the realm of possibilities. We will give many examples, in Part II, of the solutions that have been formulated and implemented with success by servant-leaders around the world. The idea is that you will be able to see the underlying patterns and get a feeling for how you can use servant-leadership to solve problems in your own company.

The examples of business challenges are described using seven concrete dilemmas:

1. Leading versus serving
2. Rules versus exceptions
3. Parts versus the whole
4. Control versus passion
5. Specific versus diffuse
6. Short term versus long term
7. Push versus pull

DILEMMA 1:
LEADING VERSUS SERVING

Challenge

Peter Webber does not have it easy in his new function as CEO of the EMEA region (Europe, Middle East, Africa) and India for Cloverpill, an international pharmaceutical company. His most important assignment is to create a more global approach in his business. That is not simple for an organization that was previously split up by countries. Most of the old country managers from the biggest markets, including India, are sitting on his new team. Peter quickly discovers that his team members are frustrated by their diminished roles. And, as if that was not enough, the team seems to have different expectations with respect to his role as a leader. The northern Europeans want to be involved in all important decisions; the Germans, rather tellingly, value detailed job descriptions; and the managers from the Latin countries and India expect decisive action from the top with a minimum of discussion. Which management style should he, in heaven's name, use? A style that would work well with one part of the group would weaken his credibility with the other parts. A catch-22.

The Dilemma

The dilemma of "serving" versus "leading" comes closest to the original meaning of the concept of servant-leader. The question of what makes someone a leader is answered differently by different cultures. Is a strong leader someone who shows his or her power and employs top-down management? Or is it someone who listens and is in favor of a bottom-up style of management?

In terms of defining leadership, cultures divide into two broad groups: the one side thinks in terms of performance and the other side thinks in terms of attributes.

In performance-oriented cultures, leaders get their status in terms of what they have achieved, what they accomplish. Even though people achieve a certain status, it is still necessary for them to prove themselves again and again. In these cultures, the subservient are seen as those who should make an effort to make the performances successful. The Netherlands has a culture that is a good example of people being encouraged to achieve results, whereas family background is less important. Deeds of the individual, leader or servant, are what count. In this culture, status is not guaranteed. In this case, it is also quite normal to ask a leader for the reasons for doing something in a certain way.

In Western cultures, there is talk of "depersonalization" of leadership, referring to the idea that achieving team or organizational goals is more important than under whose leadership that happens. *Management by objectives* is what management guru Peter Drucker calls it.[1]

"Ascribed" status is something entirely different. This is a reflection of who the person is and the relationship that he or she has with others, with the organization, or with the society at large. In this case, there are clearly defined masters and there are servants. In a culture with ascribed status, leaders derive their status from birth, age, gender, or wealth. People with a high status do not necessarily have to do anything to earn it. They get the status automatically on the basis of who they are. This is often important, for example, in the Middle and Far East. In these cultures, power is personalized—it belongs to the leader. You would sooner do things for the leader than for pure abstract goals. *Management by subjectives* is a good expression to describe this. Leaders are evaluated for their personal attributes such as decency and charisma, and their subordinates attain status based on the quality of how they serve their leader. In these cases, titles are important to let others know the "background" that a person, leader or servant, comes from.

At the core is the question: do people see status as something that someone reaches through individual efforts, or is it something that depends on who someone *is*, such as a male elder or someone coming from a "good" family? The answers to these questions give some insights into why people in some cultures enjoy status and others do not.

The Benchmark

The difference is clearly illustrated by the following two managers, A and B, talking about the organizational structure of their company:

> A: *The most important reason to have an organizational structure is so that everyone knows who is in charge of whom.*
>
> B: *The most important reason to have an organizational structure is so that everyone knows how tasks are divided and coordinated.*

Which of the two approaches gives the best reason to have an organizational structure? The answers vary drastically from culture to culture. (See Figure 5.1.)

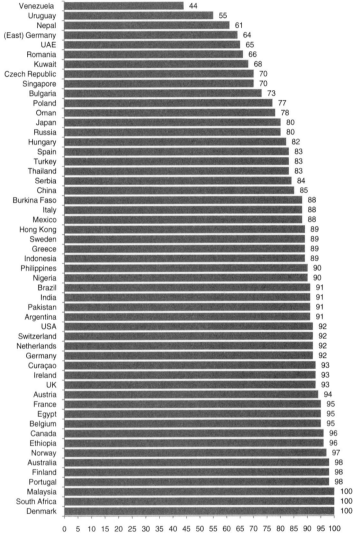

Figure 5.1 The most important reason(s) for an organizational structure (role versus task). Percentage of people that answered B.

In cultures where leaders earn their status by effectively carrying out their tasks (the performance-oriented cultures), people prefer answer B. In cultures where ascribed status is the norm, they would sooner choose A. In all cultures it is about how power is distributed, regardless of the performance of the whole.

Problems and Solutions

The difference in viewpoints in an intercultural environment ensures various dilemmas arise, for example those below:

- Master versus servant
- Autocratic versus participative leadership
- Grand design versus emergent strategy

Serving and leading seem to be two largely irreconcilable concepts, and that is what they *are*, at least for leaders who remain stuck in their own cultural point of view. A servant-leader, however, overcomes these limitations and uses them, in fact, to combine two extremes. These people will not let themselves be seduced into choosing between performance and attribution; rather, they use their status to help others to perform. This also works the other way: the performance of their team also gives them more status. In this way, performance and attribution are used in order to strengthen each other.

As you will see, there are many different ways in which to do this. Depending on culture and the personality of a leader, there can be different starting points; however, the solutions, in all their different forms, share the same theme and are manifestations of servant-leadership.

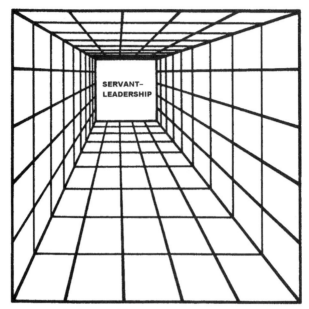

Figure 5.2 Servant-leader pyramid

Master Versus Servant

For many people, serving has a much more negative connotation than leading, as it is associated with submission. This is a misconception. A servant-leader is certainly not a carpet to be walked all over. However, you can come to the conclusion that servant-leadership is a seemingly contradictory concept.

Take a look at Figure 5.2. Is the servant-leader at the bottom of a deep shaft, or at the top of a reversed pyramid? The answer is: both. The leader has turned the organizational hierarchy around completely and serves subordinates as if they were the leader's superiors. Leaders who serve those "below" them set an example for their employees as to how they can serve the clients. If a leader does not enjoy serving others, why should the employees enjoy it? Servant-leaders try to give their status away in order to get it back with interest. The more you serve, the more you lead.

Servant-leadership has a double focus, and that opinion is shared by Jan Carlzon of SAS airlines who, in his book *Away with the Pyramids!* (coauthored by Tomas Lagerstrom), was the first to try to turn the pyramid upside down.[2] He argued that both cabin staff and bosses should serve each other as well as they served the client.

This double focus was also an important component of the radical upgrading of cabin staff service implemented at SAS and British Airways. Nick Gergades, BA's HR director in the early nineties, proposed that the cabin staff needed to serve the clients in the same way in which their superiors served them. That principle is exactly what makes servant-leadership so important. When staff members genuinely like their superiors, that shows, and an esprit de corps begins to spread, which has a positive effect on all involved.

In some cultures, servant-leadership is already deeply rooted, particularly in Asia. In Japan, for example, leaders give their followers more than they could ever repay. The result of this is that workers feel indebted to their leader, which drives them to try to fulfill the wishes of the leader. The modest character of this leadership style is a good match with Asian cultures. People with the most seniority will make the least fuss. They would rather radiate that they would like to learn something from you. This modesty works to actually increase their status. A Japanese leader is, in this way, the perfect example of the integration of master and servant, coming in from the serving perspective.

Autocratic Versus Participative Leadership

As a leader, do you rely on authority or participation of your employees? The choice you make is extremely important. In Figure 5.3, you can see where authoritarian and partici-

Figure 5.3 Degree of authority versus degree of participation

pative leadership can lead and which variations thereof are possible.

On the vertical axis, the leader's authority is shown. In its most extreme, the consequence is a power trip. As Lord Acton said, *"Power tends to corrupt and absolute power corrupts absolutely."* [3] On the horizontal axis is the level of participation. Taken to the extreme, allowing for the involvement of others can result in a leadership crisis because the authority is disputed by those who are supposed to be led by the leader. It can end in chaos and rebellion, as those who were being led take the lead. This actually took place when the Pilgrim Fathers, on their way to the New World, mutinied against the captain while still at sea.

Between random and failed leadership, there is the transactional leader, a typical case of compromise. Transactional leaders see life as a large transaction, a simple conducting of business. The transactional leader is tolerated because he or she ensures the paycheck, and the employee delivers routine work for routine pay. Nothing new is created and each party is working in its own favor.

In the upper right of the figure, you see the transformational leader, who "stands on the shoulders of giants" and, because of the experience, is capable of so much more. Transformational leadership—another name for servant-leadership—is all about change. The leader changes the consciousness of those being led by identifying desires that were previously unconscious. In the same way, they change the consciousness of the leader. Well-known transformational leaders include Franklin D. Roosevelt, Gandhi, Martin Luther King Jr., and Nelson Mandela.

Transformational leaders are also present in corporations today. Such a man is Laurent Beaudoin, who transformed Bombardier from a skimobile company to a transportation and aeronautic company, a significant increase in complexity. Richard Branson imprinted his personality on the portfolio of the Virgin Companies. Gergei Kiriyenko, the youngest prime minister of Russia ever, transformed NORSi Oil from an apathetic, bankrupted organization that was paralyzed with fear into a living, dynamic, and effective company.

In this variation, both elements, authoritarian and participative, are present in their full glory in such a way that they strengthen each other. This is a typical sort of servant-leader solution. Transformational leadership is known for its two-way direction, which is an important aspect of servant-leadership. Servant-leaders and their followers anticipate each other's behavior and are dependent on one another in a healthy manner. The fact that people have put their faith in their leader and identify with him or her is as important for the leader as for the led. The boundaries between the two fade as people feel lifted up in a wave of connection and shared goals.

Grand Design Versus Emergent Strategy

We have the Canadian Henry Mintzberg to thank for the categorization of several strategic approaches. Mintzberg named the top-down approach of the old power model *grand design*. This is the practice whereby you plot the next steps for the next battle far from the battlefield, without having detailed knowledge of the circumstances, of what is actually going on at the front. The result: many dead and wounded. Another approach is to use the experience of soldiers (bottom-up). In this form, strategy arises from the experience gained in the field and is referred to as the *emergent strategy* by Mintzberg.[4]

This is sometimes thought, incorrectly, to be a characteristic of servant-leadership. The servant-leader should create situations in which the strategies of others can come to light. In reality, that is rarely the case. A sign of a servant-leader is that he or she does not make a choice between the two points of view, but unites them. This is what Mintzberg calls a *crafting strategy*.[5] Here we see top-down and bottom-up strategies as text in context. He or she develops the *why* inside of which the concrete experiences from the field have more context. The servant-leader ensures a constant connection between experience and learning and tests these according to the planned next steps.

You often see that the "hands-on" sales departments have difficulty with the more "theoretic" and distant marketing department. The sales agents work with clients every day and have more face-to-face contact. The marketing department, on the other hand, is much more conceptual and looks at the market reality from inside the office. Servant-leaders make sure that the many *trial-and-error* experiences in sales are bundled together within the strategic perspective of marketing. Marketing in turn makes sure that the "grand design" forms the context for and gives meaning to the "emergent" activities of the sales team.

A perfect example of this is how, over the past several years, Unilever has been able to cut the number of its individual brands in half by listening closely to what the sales departments had to say.

Different Starting Points

Servant-leadership works in cultures because it has different starting points.

For example, an American company in financial services bought a significant share of a Chinese bank. Part of the deal was to train the top 1,000 Chinese managers, who went to a two-week course. On the last day, they were invited to share their perspectives about the intercultural aspects of policy and the possible adaptations thereof in China. The question arose about the usefulness of the American participative training methods. Is a training method that is based on participation possible in a culture in which people are used to one-way communication and where the expression of your opinion at a lower level is *not done* because it is related to the risk of the leader's losing face? Is servant-leadership even possible in such a culture?

The answer is yes, but servant-leadership in an Eastern culture will have a different starting point from in the West. It is obvious that the Chinese will not likely come to the point where they give their opinion *en plein publique* as the Americans are used to. It was, however, possible to combine the two extremes—authority and participation— in a creative way.

The solution was that the Chinese leaders used their authority to get the participation of their colleagues by directing that they should give their opinions in small groups. By reducing the number of participants per group, the fear of loss of face was lessened and the Chinese colleagues dared to say more.

What a difference there is with servant-leadership in northern Europe! There, servant-leaders have an entirely different starting point, especially considering the fact that the members of their teams are used to giving their points of view. In these cultures, it is an art not to get people to participate, but to make sure they follow the direction set by the leader. A Dutch manager explained that he was struggling with the latter problem in his organization. It took so much energy to get his employees to accept his decision and to consensually act on it. He was advised to ask them what they needed the most. The answer was unanimous: strong and clear leadership!

Conclusion

The servant-leader will get more authority to lead by serving, will use his or her top-down approach to better listen to bottom-up concerns, and will look at the big picture in a strategic way in order to mold strategies that emerge into a meaningful whole.

The examples above make it clear that leaders in every culture are struggling with the same dilemmas but that the way in which they deal with the problem is determined by culture. This is an important insight. The literature on servant-leadership does suggest that the starting point is by serving. In light of intercultural leadership, however, it is rarely understood that this is a Western view. Currently, most internationally known authors and experienced professionals in this field come from the West, which is why they are so used to thinking from a power model, and why it seems that the logical first step is to start with serving and go in the direction of the other style.

It is also typically Western to assume that a servant-leader represents the pyramid on its head. This is generally right, but a servant-leader will also make sure that the pyramid is set right again with the broad bottom as a base. In times of crisis, when a top-down approach is necessary, a servant-leader will take the reins, and that is what is expected of him or her. For leaders in an Eastern culture, serving is the status quo; the real challenge is in strengthening their leadership.

This is the case in practice. It takes two weeks of training to teach an American flight attendant how to appear to enjoy serving passengers. This is in stark contrast to flight attendant from Singapore Airlines or, indeed, from Southwest, where Colleen Barrett brought in the concept of servant-leadership years ago. In their case, the notion of serving seems to sit in their cultural DNA.

Employees from both are formed by their cultures and bring these with them to work. For the American flight attendant, serving is an area of development, while the Chinese colleague would need to give extra attention to personal leadership qualities. For a servant-leader, it does not matter where the circle begins. Some leaders are busy for the first fifty years of their lives gathering enough authority to be seen as a leader. During the following ten or twenty years, the leader uses this authority to serve. Others have served for years in order to become a leader in a later stage. Whatever the starting point, the servant-leader is about two-way traffic and mutual dependence, because dependence as a pure servant is not sustainable, just as top-down power is not. A servant-leader always starts from his or her own strength and quickly thereafter shifts to the other side that needs to be developed.

Resolution

And what does all of this mean for Peter Webber? What now would make him a servant-leader who is considered to have an effective approach when it comes to intercultural differences? His preference is to get everyone involved in decisions so that, later, in the implementation stage, he does not have any problems. But those from the Middle East and the Latin countries will think that this is nonsense. A leader has guts and makes decisions. Peter Webber must, above all, be authentic and not deny his natural character. Then, to begin, he needs to listen long and hard. That works, in every culture. Afterward, he needs to process the information and, together with a few trusted advisers, come to a decision that he then presents as decided. In other words, Peter serves his team best by listening first and then, armed with the necessary information, demonstrating strong leadership.

Notes

1   Peter F. Drucker, *The Effective Executive* (New York: Harper & Row, 1967).

2   *Away with the Pyramids!* is the translated title of the Swedish book by Jan Carlzon and Tomas Lagerstrom, *Riv Pyramiderna!: En Bok Om Den Nya Manniskan, Chefen Och Ledaren* (Sweden: Bonnier, 1985).

3   Lord Acton expressed this opinion in a letter to Bishop Mandell Creighton in 1887.

4   H. Mintzberg, "Patterns in Strategy Formation," *Management Science*, Vol. 24, No. 9, 1978.

5   Henry Mintzberg, "Crafting Strategy," *Harvard Business Review* (Boston: Harvard Business Review Press, July 1987).

DILEMMA 2:
RULES VERSUS EXCEPTIONS

Challenge

Peter Webber holds his head in his hands. What does globalization mean exactly for a region like EMEA where his company is active? There is a huge difference in markets, local traditions, and culture between northern and southern Europe, let alone the Middle East, Africa, and India. How can you have a uniform management style, or is this even desirable? Should he focus on his team's responsibility for the entire EMEA area or for the local markets? Is it realistic to use northern Europe as a standard to measure other regions and countries? Or is there something in the arguments of Giovanni and Arun, that Italy and India have unique characteristics that Peter needs to deal with separately? Peter Webber wrestles with the same dilemma that international companies face: the dilemma between rules and exceptions. He has been interested in servant-leadership for years. The theory made sense to him, but translating that theory into daily practice is still a quest. In this specific case, what would be a typical servant-leader solution?

The Dilemma

Every leader has to deal with rules, laws, commitments and generalizations, uniformity and conformity. At the same time, every leader knows the importance of relationships, differences, uniqueness, exceptions, and differentiating elements.

While some cultures strive for rules that apply to everyone, other cultures are more concerned with exceptions and specific cases. Many American companies are interested in globalizing but want to maintain standards from headquarters. They ask themselves, how can we get everyone to stay? On the other side there are cultures that start with the reverse and specifically value the exceptional and unique product, such as food for the French and Japanese, fashion for the Italian, and invention for the researcher.

In the tension that exists between different cultures it is important for the leader to use exceptions in order to ensure better rules, and to have rules that can be used in exceptional situations. It is by combining the extremes that a leader serves.

There are cultures that believe that general rules, codes, values, and standards should take priority over individual needs and claims from friends and relatives. In societies that are based on this principle, the same rules apply for everyone. Exceptions weaken the rule. In these cultures it is obvious that you should tell the truth, even if it harms yourself, your boss, a friend, or anyone else, and you should be honest with insurance companies and tax offices rather than being "creative" with the truth. The idea that people in the same situations should be handled the same way according to the law is a value deeply rooted in many Western countries. That is not to say that individual circumstances have no effect on tipping the scales one way or the other. They will definitely be considered, but specifically in respect to the universal rule.

This also does not imply that, in these cultures, relationships do not matter. Friends and family are definitely important. But the universal truth—the law—is simply above these relationships.

In cultures that give preference to exceptions and specific situations, the opposite is true. People in these cultures see the ideal society in terms of friendship, unusual situations, and a network of intimate relationships. The spirit of the law is more important than the letter of the law. Of course, these cultures have rules and laws, but they govern mostly how people deal with each other. Rules are necessary, if only in order to make exceptions in certain cases. However, in general, you should always be able to count on the support of your friends in these cultures.

The Benchmark

In order to measure how people in different countries think about the value of rules and exceptions, more than 80,000 people around the world were presented with the following case:

> *Imagine that you are a food critic and you are eating at a new restaurant in order to write an article for the paper. It is not the most positive experience: the food, the drink, and even the service are below standard. At the end of the evening, a good friend of yours comes out of the kitchen and tells you that he has taken his entire savings and put it into this restaurant. What do you do? Do you tell*

the truth, even if that harms your friend (professional standard), or do you protect your friend, even at the cost of the truth? In other words, do you choose your professional standard or your unique friendship? Where is your highest responsibility? This case brings many of the deepest cultural differences to light.

This hypothetical case clearly illustrates the importance of the point of view from which people operate. The diversity in answers is enormous. People around the world react differently to this example, as can be seen in Figure 6.1.

In cultures where the rules are very important, such as Australia, the United States, Switzerland, and Finland, most people choose the truth, opting for an objective article being published in the paper about the terrible quality of the restaurant. In cultures that place strong value on exceptions, such as China, Korea, and Russia, most people would make an exception in this special case, and write a partially true, but totally positive, article for their friend, even if that means going against their professional standards.

Problems and Solutions

If people all over the world react differently to a hypothetical story, then it will come as no surprise that it happens all the time in daily life, leading to many misunderstandings. Everyone reacts from his or her own perspective and therefore clashes with colleagues who operate from a different perspective are not infrequent. It makes a good deal of difference whether you follow universal rules or you prefer to pay attention to specific circumstances and behave accordingly. The debate over "rules or exceptions" can apply to a wide

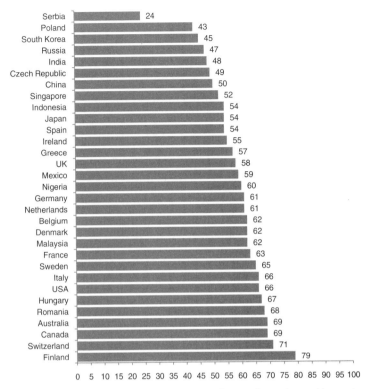

Figure 6.1 The restaurant dilemma. Percentage of respondents who would not write a false review and do not believe their friend has a right to expect them to help.

variety of situations. It includes questions like: Should we globalize or focus locally? Should we go for mass production or specialized products? Should we just follow the universal company standards or should we listen to the individual on the work floor and take advantage of a special case?

This can lead to the following dilemmas:

- Fatal error versus chance to improve
- Legal contracts versus free interpretations
- Universal criteria versus unique ideas
- Global versus local

Fatal Error Versus Chance to Improve

Dealing with mistakes is territory where servant-leadership is especially visible. A process controller at Motorola once tried to improve the cleaning process of the electrical circuits of GSMs. Because he used brushes that were too sharp, he not only cleaned more of the debris away but also cut through important circuits. The result was more than a hundred thousand dollars in damage. When he was invited to CEO Bob Galvin's office, he prepared himself to be fired. To his surprise, Bob Galvin asked him to write a report about how they could permanently avoid similar mistakes in the future. After reading the report, Galvin announced that the employee and his analysis were responsible for a new cleaning approach that saved the organization more than a million dollars.

After a hundred-thousand-dollar mistake like that, most CEOs would have fired the employee on the spot. Not Bob Galvin; he illustrated an important principle of servant-leadership: the view that mistakes are chances for improvement. Leadership is only effective if you create an *error-correcting* system that continually learns from unusual mistakes. In the long term, there is nothing more deadly than a perfect system, a wedding without disagreements, or a car without defects. You can only judge the service of a car the moment that there is a defect. Of course, the defect should remain an exception, but the reaction to the special situation opens a world of possibilities for the auto dealer to differentiate itself from the competition.

The servant-leader will always try to view the mistakes of others as chances to learn and grow. That is why he or she asks the useful questions: What can we learn from this mistake? What can we do next time to make sure it does not happen again? How can we limit the damage that the mistake caused? Edward Deming, the quality guru, even goes so far as to say that mistakes are a requirement for the improved quality of production.

Legal Contracts Versus Free Interpretations

One of the most common dilemmas is the tension between strict rules and free interpretations. Uniformity applies to the first, creativity to the second. The two poles are difficult to reconcile. That was demonstrated at the Shell Laboratory in Amsterdam where researchers often complained about the system of role evaluation with which they had to work. For every position, there was a detailed description of what was necessary in terms of knowledge, capability to solve problems, and responsibilities. This attention to detail and following the rules to the nth degree was fatal for their creativity; also, because change is inherent in research, and because these documents took a long time to prepare, the job descriptions were outdated in no time.

That raised the question of whether such a static rule- and procedure-oriented instrument was actually suited for a dynamic breeding ground. The answer is definitely yes, as long as you view both sides positively and search for a synthesis.

On the one side, you are dealing with the quickly changing research culture, while on the other side, there is a need for consistency between roles, both international and within the company. In order to do right by both extremes, the role descriptions were written a bit more abstractly. By describing three kinds of researchers at three different levels, 1,200 people could be included in just nine job descriptions. Points were awarded based on this description, and the person's manager had to demonstrate that the person complied with the criteria. As a result, the system was less vulnerable to change. The strict management made it clear that under no condition was it to be made public that an exception had been made for the research department. It was therefore remarkable to see that just five years later, the entire Shell Group had made this smart method of benchmarking the organization-wide standard. Servant-leadership is only effective between two cultures when it reconciles two opposing orientations to a higher level.

Universal Criteria Versus Unique Ideas

The quality of a servant-leader, that of his or her team, and that of the interaction between both is the most important set of factors for determining the success of an organization. There are thousands of books written about both subjects, and justly so.

One of the most original thinkers about the subject of management teams is the British author and consultant Meredith Belbin. In his first book, *Management Teams*, he described how the gifted Apollo Team performed significantly worse than the second team, which consisted of fewer individually talented members but that worked better together as a team.[1] According to Belbin, an effective team is a group of people who strive for a common goal and, in the process, go through certain phases. We will describe several of these in the next chapter. After almost forty years of research, he came to the conclusion that the effectiveness of a team depends on the fulfillment of eight roles.

The creation of wealth is often realized by complementary roles within an organization or a society. The success of a team requires that the roles are held by one or more of its members. This immediately gives a deeper meaning to the term *diversity.*

The identification of and distinguishing between these roles is only the beginning. The role of a servant-leader is to reconcile the fundamental differences between the individual team roles and assert a positive influence on the relationship between those roles.

In the first phase of team development, defining the task, Belbin makes a distinction between the role of the unorthodox *Plant,* who comes up with creative ideas, and the *Monitor-Evaluator,* who contributes his or her fair share of distant and careful critique. He or she critically evaluates the ideas of the team and does problem analysis. As you can see in Figure 6.2, it is necessary to take a critical look at the Plant in order to avoid building castles in the sky. On the other hand, if the Monitor-Evaluator holds sway, there are no more ideas left over.

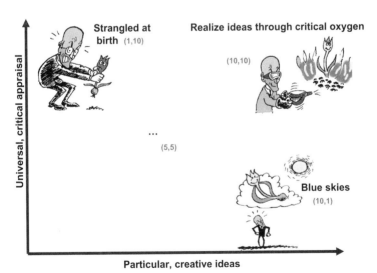

Figure 6.2 Universal criteria versus unique ideas; Belbin's Monitor-Evaluator and Plant team roles

Both extremes are unproductive. There is nothing more fatal for innovation in a team than having one consisting of only creative people. Therefore, Belbin operated according to two important game rules. First, criticism must be constructive. If you immediately crush an idea because, for example, there is not money available for it, you run the risk of throwing the baby out with the bathwater. It makes much more sense to agree that you will give criticism to an idea only after you have first also given two good things about the idea. This increases the chances of not missing a truly brilliant idea. The second rule is that criticism can only be given in the form of a question, specifically: How can I help you to solve the problem with your idea? This method is called *synectics*. Thanks to this method, the rules for criticism are bent just enough for unique ideas to get a chance. And it works. As a result of synectics, teams are notably more innovative and creative.

Global Versus Local

Many international companies have trouble with the question of what should have priority: rules from the head office or unique situations on the local work floor? Something can be said for both, but it is difficult because the decision for one shuts out the good aspects of the other. Or should you do a little bit of both, even though it is just a weak compromise?

The servant-leader takes a different path, a path that leads past the choice for a compromise to a more productive approach. This path starts with a positive view of culture differences. According to intercultural specialist Milton Bennett, there are varying phases of intercultural sensitivity, from ethnocentrism to ethnorelativism.[2] Servant-leaders always operate from an ethnorelativist point of view. That means that they view the relative cultural differences in a healthy way and deal with them positively; the more sensitive they are, the more advantage they can get out of cultural diversity.

International and Multinational Organizations

The servant-leader will always try to use local best practices and implement them globally. In the same way, he or she will decide to what extent the quality of the global offering can be used in a local context. The servant-leader must have a highly developed competence in dealing with cultural differences.

Milton Bennett developed a model in which he defines six phases of intercultural sensitivity. The more sensitive a leader is, the more likely the leader is to make the most of cultural diversity. The first three phases are ethnocentric, meaning that people unconsciously view their own culture as the center of their reality. And that is the last thing that a servant-leader would do. The most banal form of ethnocentricity is the first phase: *Denial.* In this phase, leaders cannot recognize cultural differences, let alone experience them. There are no alternatives to their own logic, and if there are, they are inferior. These are the managers like the ones you meet in the Midwest of the United States that insist, "If everyone just learns to speak English, there won't be any cultural problems." These are the same people who have never experienced culture shock, as opposed to the people all around them who have. Their solution to cultural difference is to isolate or leave the other alone, like in the times of apartheid. These managers not only do not know other cultures but also have no idea about their own. They lack experience with differences, which is essential in order to gain an insight into your own situation.

The second ethnocentric phase is that of *Defensiveness*. Here, the world is divided into "us" against "them," and this "other" is always inferior. In this case, we are talking about the internationalizing managers who are convinced that their organization (and the knowledge they have) is superior. Local differences are not really valued.

When the threat of the Defensive phase is diminished through the understanding that all people are intrinsically the same, then you enter the third phase, that of *Minimizing*. This is the point you are at when talking about the so-called global organization. In such an organization, it is generally recognized that there are cultural differences, and these are also tolerated, but a strong organizational culture (such as that at IBM, Exxon, HP, and GE) ensures that there is movement in the direction of conformity. Similar companies are known for the old "power culture." It is "my way or the highway" when operating in a global organization.

The first phase of ethnorelativism is *Acceptance*. Through long-lasting international contact, leaders understand that they have their own cultural context, which, to some extent, determines their behavior and that there are other cultures that ascribe different meanings to their lives. These organizations see the value in cultural diversity and give serious attention to attracting employees from different cultures. Top management is rarely made up only of individuals from the country where the head office is located. This results in international organizations such as Walt Disney. The culture of the corporate headquarters is clearly centralized, yet at the local level in Paris it is more decentralized, with adjustments for the local market, such as selling wine at Disneyland Paris.

The second ethnorelativist phase is *Adjustment*, with multinational organizations as the concrete result. Leaders in these organizations are ready and willing to look at the world from different points of view. They also easily adapt themselves to a wide variety of local circumstances. KPMG is a good example of such a multinational company. Multinational managers believe, from experience, that when in Rome, one must do as the Romans do. You can recognize these organizations from the abundance of language courses they offer and the traditional cross-cultural programs such as "Doing Business with the Japanese."

Transcultural Organizations

Finally, there are transcultural organizations with a hyper-culture, such as Pearle Optical, Sematech, and Applied Materials. These organizations have begun the last phase: full *Integration*. This is the phase in which the connection between the two extremes is made successfully. You can no longer do as the Romans do because Rome no longer exists. These organizations are like diamonds—you can no longer tell which is the top. (See Figure 6.3.)

This can lead to unusual organizational constructions. For example, Pearle Optical only has ten people at the head office in Amsterdam who run a number of Centers of Excellence across Europe, varying from R&D to Marketing. This is only possible within the context of servant-leadership because they have the competence to look for unusual and unique solutions that can only be found at a local level, and

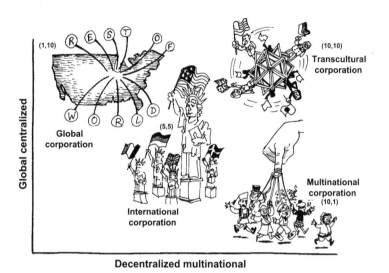

Figure 6.3 Centralized versus decentralized

at the same time, they learn best practices, which they then spread across the entire company.

Sematech, the International Institute for Semiconductors, has a different approach. Sematech was an American initiative, meant to compete against the quickly developing economies of Southeast Asia. At Sematech, American companies worked closely to beat Japanese and Korean competitors. The cooperation between former rivals Intel, AMD, and National Semiconductor was so successful that, in just five years, they almost wiped away the international competition. The strategy worked, and the most exceptional part about it was, at the moment of success, instead of discontinuing the cooperation, it was expanded! Former competitors in Europe, Philips and Siemens joined, and in Asia, Samsung and Sony were invited to join the group. They all heartily accepted the invitation. This is an example of how competition can lead to cooperation. We speak of a *transcultural* organization because of the manner in which servant-leaders do business by effectively integrating tensions, such as competition and teamwork, local and global, irrespective of the culture where it is applied.

Hyperculture

Applied Materials has found another way to get the best out of cultural diversity. This company makes sure that the global rules are watertight by encouraging people with different viewpoints to make them. Concretely this means that the top management team consists of seven different nationalities (nine, if you count double nationalities). The organization is run by several different Centers of Excellence, also outside the United States. Because all international activities are done in multicultural teams, all the managers are used to switching from one to another international context. Those who move from one culture to another no longer see themselves as egos in the center. They often use the intersections between cultures as a platform to develop a *hyperculture* that rises above differences and makes the best of them.

Individual cultures focus on themselves and are often exclusive—literally shutting others out. The hyperculture, what Charles Hampden-Turner calls *reconciled values,*[3] is made up of all the diverse and exclusive identities, but on a higher level, where they come together and strengthen one another. The creation of a hyperculture is therefore significantly enriching. It is an organizational culture known for servant-leadership, the form of leadership that brings people with different points of view out of the resulting tension and is able to channel it into a productive dynamic.

Another typical sign of hyperculture is that the leader is explicit about his or her core values: respect for differences is a shared starting point.

Conclusion

Leaders create a culture. Managers create a monoculture. Servant-leaders create a hyperculture. There are many ways to do the latter. In one case, the servant-leader may focus on successful local practices in order to extrapolate these to a global policy. Imagine that an important innovation happens in France. Then it is relevant for you as a leader to ask yourself if this innovation is applicable globally. If that is the case, the local practice brings the quality of global service to a higher level. In another case, he or she may ensure that the global rule is of a high quality because it is made by people of different cultural backgrounds. In both cases, the challenge is to make rules better with the help of exceptions.

Resolution

And what does this mean now for Peter Webber? What is the answer to the typical servant-leadership approach to the dilemma between global rules and local exceptions in his company?

The most important process that he as a servant-leader has to set into motion is the combining of starting points: the universal truth at the head office with the uniqueness of the local situation. Servant-leaders bring points of view together. In this way, they lay the basis for the bridging of differences, and the solution comes by itself. It is interesting to note that for a long time there was no word in

Japanese for objectivity. *Eventually, they took the Chinese characters over for the following word:* kyakkanteki. *This means "the point of view of the outsider." The opposite is* shukanteki: *"the point of view of the insider." Servant-leadership gives both points of view the chance to be heard. The servant-leader is like a gardener in a Japanese garden that is designed to give people different views of reality.*

Notes

1   Meredith R. Belbin, *Management Teams: Why They Succeed or Fail* (London: Butterworth Heinemann, 2nd edition, 2004).
2   Milton J. Bennett, "Towards a Developmental Model of Intercultural Sensitivity," in R. Michael Paige, ed., *Education for the Intercultural Experience* (Yarmouth, ME: Intercultural Press, 1993).
3   Charles Hampden-Turner, *Charting the Corporate Mind: Graphic Solutions to Business Conflicts* (New York: The Free Press, 1990).

DILEMMA 3:
PARTS VERSUS THE WHOLE

Challenge

Besides his responsibilities for EMEA, Peter Webber also sometimes has to work with the international organization of Cloverpill. A few years ago, Cloverpill decided to internationalize its operations. During the first phase of operations, some important departments, such as R&D, had been moved from the Midwest (USA) to France, renowned for its excellent education in the field of chemicals. On the other hand, sales were especially promising in the Asian "Tiger Economies" and in the United States, in contrast to declining sales in EMEA. During the last management meeting in Chicago, Peter spoke about the need for more consistency between Cloverpill Inc. and EMEA.

In the past, the Europeans worked in Europe and the Americans worked in the United States, but due to internationalization of the market, there are more and more multicultural teams, and intercontinental mobility is greater than ever.

The American HR manager proposed initiating a proven, individualistic incentive system worldwide to increase the productivity of the entire staff. This system

---

had been proven successful in the United States. However, Peter foresaw some difficulties with how the introduction of an individualized bonus system would clash with the EMEA culture, where team orientation is more dominant. Moreover, he had just spent a lot of time and effort adjusting the HR system to recognize this difference. He would need to make a decision soon, but what would be the wise thing to do?

The Dilemma

Margaret Mead, a famous anthropologist, once said, "A small group of thoughtful people can change the world. Indeed, it's the only thing that ever has." The quality of a leader, of a team, and of the interaction between both is the most important indicator of success for an organization. It is about connecting the diverse parts with the whole. Here, the servant-leader plays an important part. In individualistic cultures, it is best for the servant-leader to take as a starting point the importance of individual independence and creativity, and then use these for the benefit of the group. In a more communitarian culture, a servant-leader will have a different point of departure. Here, he or she will look at the dilemma from the perspective of the larger group and subsequently ask, "How can the group's interests stimulate individual freedom and innovation?"

In predominantly individualistic cultures, the individual is positioned against the collective. The individual determines the norm. His or her well-being, happiness, and sense of satisfaction are of the utmost importance. It is expected that the individual will act primarily in his or her own interest. People's first responsibility is to themselves and to their direct family. They derive status based on their own achievements. The quality of life for all of society's members is closely connected with the opportunities for individual independence and development, and the community is judged according to the extent to which it serves the interests of its individual members. Examples of cultures where individualism is more predominant include the United Kingdom and the United States of America.

The power of individualistic cultures lies primarily in their sense of self-confidence and the space they give to the individual. In these cultures, individuals get the chance to bloom and achieve unique results. People are encouraged to try new things. This creates an environment where business can flourish. Another strong point about these cultures is that they generally can handle different minority points of view, as well as critical commentary. Freedom of expression is an important societal value. Of the world's individualistic cultures, the United States is known as *the* champion of freedom. Just as Americans are not afraid to promote their values worldwide, they are not afraid of the unknown.

At the other end of the spectrum, you find that communitarian cultures value the group over the individual. In these cultures, the most important responsibility of the individuals is to conduct themselves in a way that serves the collective. The quality of life of the individual is directly related to the degree to which he or she takes care of the other members of society, even if this is at a cost to his or her own freedom. People are judged on how much they serve the needs of the group. Both in China and in Japan, working as a team and contributing to the collective is of higher importance than individual accomplishment or success.

The positive quality of communitarian cultures is their emphasis on looking beyond individual interests. This leads to support for the less fortunate and the notion that the strongest shoulders carry the heaviest loads. These cultures are strong in connecting diverging areas such as business, education, finance, and politics in a sensible way. In addition, they are aware of the fact that they are the caretakers of the earth for future generations and, therefore, are more frugal with the earth's resources. Also they are good at creating an esprit de corps. Finally, companies in these societies tend to promote the health and education of their employees, resulting in a high level of involvement, productivity, and quality.

Double Focus

Though there are demonstrable differences between the two cultures, this does not mean that people in individualistic cultures are preoccupied with themselves or that people in a communitarian society are concerned about everyone but themselves. In all cultures, people are a part of greater social networks. They are members of a family, a neighborhood or town, a football club, or a company. Individualism and communitarianism coexist in all communities; only the predominance or emphasis differs substantially. No one is completely free of social pressure, and on the other hand, no one is completely tied down by social responsibilities. Companies operate daily between these two tensions. Attention to the individual and the group is both valuable and necessary. It is thus not a question of "either-or"; rather, the key question is: Where is your first priority? Is this with yourself or the group?

An individual needs a community from which to derive his or her significance, while the community exists solely through the contributions of a great many people. One is not better than the other. Both have more positive and less positive aspects. The point is to find a position in which each side strengthens the other. Rather than see individualism and communitarianism in opposition, it is better to see them as two parts of the whole.

The importance of being able to integrate the two horns of a dilemma is significant. Take, for example, a family where children leave the house at sixteen or seventeen years of age, never to return, or even call home. You might then say to your partner, "Perhaps we helped develop their sense of individual autonomy too much." On the other hand, if your son is forty-two years old and says, "Father, I am so happy to still live with you here at home," then you may have spent too much time fostering the other side of the duality. Effective parents succeed when they have brought their children up to be both autonomous and a part of the family. Generally, rewards for behavior are based on achieving this. Parents will give their children a pat on the back if they do something positive for their brothers or sisters, and the family, as a whole, will be lauded if they produce truly authentic children. These are "servant-parents."

The Benchmark

The two positions above lie miles apart. At the center of this dilemma is a difference of opinion as to which ensures "quality of life." To illustrate this difference, 100,000 people were asked to answer the question, "How can you increase the quality of your life?" They were presented with two statements to choose from:

> A: *It is obvious that if one has as much freedom as possible and the maximum opportunity to develop oneself, the quality of one's life would improve as a result.*

B: *If the individual is continuously taking care of his or her fellows, then the quality of life for us all will improve, even if it obstructs individual freedom and individual development.*

There were considerable differences in the answers. The responses varied along cultural lines and clearly coincided with cultural trends, as shown in Figure 7.1.

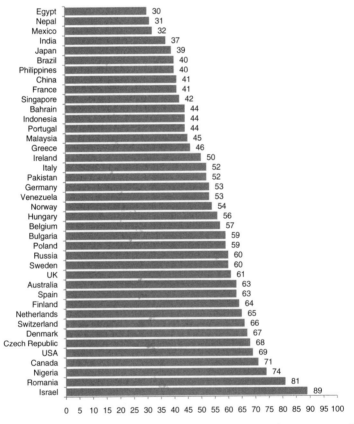

Figure 7.1 Parts (individuals) versus the whole (the group). Percentage of respondents who choose individual freedom.

Problems and Solutions

Sometimes, the interest of the individual can be juxtaposed with the interests of the team. In these cases, should the individual accommodate the desires of the group or should the team provide greater freedom to the lone individual? In a business context, a similar question might be: Should managers focus on the development, enrichment, and achievement of the individual employee and shareholders or should they focus on profit to the organization, the clients, and the greater good?

This dilemma has many aspects. There follows a number of problems and solutions from business practice:

- Competition versus cooperation
- Individual versus team rewards
- Rival disciplines versus agreement in the business plan
- Process of consensus versus realization of mature product

Competition Versus Cooperation

In a small harbor near a peninsula in England, where several streams and small waterways meet up with each other, there are many independent water taxis operating. They all offered "River Trips" in order to survive off the limited income that tourism provides. Although they compete with each other for clients, when it comes to providing supplementary services and coordinating schedules, they work together. In the local brochure they advertise themselves as "Independent Operators Working Together."

There is a good chance that this particular solution was thought of by a servant-leader. Such a person knows how to create an effective team from creative individuals, as well as the reverse: how to make the team responsible for supporting creative talents of the individual group members, working together to reach the best solution for the whole. This approach has also been called "co-opetition." As the name suggests, this approach unites the best of two worlds: cooperation and competition.

Individual Versus Team Rewards

An excellent example of this involves the advice of author and consultant Mr. Gallway, given to IBM's sales force. Instead of giving the biggest bonus to the person who sold the most computers, a practice that discourages sharing of information between members of the sales staff, Gallway recommended an alternative that rewarded both the salespeople and the clients. To be eligible for a bonus, salespeople had to make a presentation to each other every quarter about what they had learned from their clients. As a result of this initiative, sales rose by 25 percent, the clients were happy, and there was an exchange of information between sales staff. This is also an example of co-opetition: competing to cooperate with the client. An interesting outcome of this exercise was that the highest sellers turned out to be the ones who had learned the most from their clients.

The idea that there is a relationship between motivation of an individual and of the team has consequences for reward systems. As an example, an American company introduced an interesting way of recognizing achievements by the creation of a system based on a 50 percent variable reward, including options, which only became valuable for those who stayed with the company for at least three years. This approach reconciled short- and long-term thinking, and people were highly motivated by the idea that their achievements had an effect on the organization.

In Europe and Asia this reward system generated quite a lot of resistance. In Europe, the difficulty was due to certain fiscal limitations, but in Asia, it was not obvious why the system did not work. It seemed so simple: If you are in America, you apply a personal reward system. In Asia, you win people over by using the team reward system. Finally, in Europe you do everything to avoid taxes. Simple, right? However, it is not as simple as it seems. Such a decentralized approach works well enough in a multinational organization, but for a transnational organization with multicultural teams, the reward system will need to be adjusted to accommodate the greater diversity of the team.

Let's go back for a minute to the prickly problem of Peter Webber. How can he create a reward system that will constructively bring Moroccan, American, Japanese, and Dutch employees together? Moroccans and Japanese are traditionally raised to be more group oriented while American and Dutch managers are more accustomed to measure individuals against each other. Obviously, then, for the Americans and the Dutch, it is easier to accept that the one who produces the most results wins the highest bonus. This approach, however, does little to promote cooperation with the Moroccans and the Japanese.

The process of internationalization requires a new kind of logic and a new approach to management and reward systems. Obviously, there are many approaches that are unsuccessful. One of these is to ask all the employees to take a course on individual responsibility in order to be accountable for their own creativity. On a group level this is called "individualization of the community." The problem remains that "individualized" people do not readily share information.

Another (non-)solution would be to choose a remuneration system only for team spirit. The Japanese are very good at developing a sense of team. However, an overemphasis on the importance of the team can lead to a collective mediocrity. The worst option is a compromise where there is no integration: to reward small teams, with half the reward going to the individual and the other half going to the team, for example. With this approach, both the individual and the team are not properly recognized for their contribution, and thus become demotivated. But what, then, is a good solution?

Let's look again at the example of Sematech discussed earlier. In that example, strategic cooperation led to the impressive revival of an industry that was on its "deathbed." The approach they took was a classic example of "co-opetition": cooperate to compete. The associated companies were focused on transforming groups of creative individualists into teams where they could exceed themselves individually.

It worked, and you can see the result depicted in Figure 7.2.

Shell also tried something similar at the end of the eighties. In an experiment with 2,000 people from the R&D division, the company tried to integrate the talents of creative individual researchers from various countries through teamwork. For a period of one year, a 20 percent variable was divided equally over the individual and the team bonuses. The individual bonus went to the person who was chosen as the best team player. The team bonus went to the team that most excelled at supporting individual creativity. In this way, the Shell researchers competed for the best cooperation and they worked together to compete better.

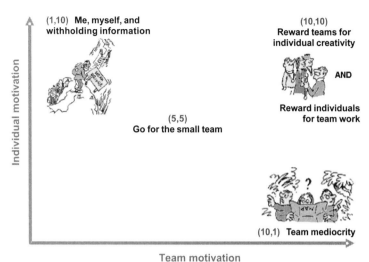

Figure 7.2 Co-opetition: cooperation reconciled with competition

Rival Disciplines Versus Agreement in the Business Plan

The Specialist Versus the Coordinator

In the previous chapter, we referred to Belbin's theories regarding how different roles are needed in the teams, and the tensions that these can create. The example we focused on was the tension between the creative Plant and the critical and analytical Monitor-Evaluator.

With respect to the dilemma of "parts versus the whole," there is another Belbin pairing that is of importance, namely the *Specialist* and the *Coordinator*. These two come into the picture once the original idea has gone through the initial testing, and the commercial idea is born. This then needs to be translated into a business plan. Specialists are experts in particular areas essential to the project or product. However, they only make individual contributions regarding their small part of the project or product and often get stuck in the technical details, without regard to the practical applicability. The Coordinator has to ensure that their ideas reach the team and that diverse areas of knowledge are integrated. Considering their contrasting objectives, the relationship between the Coordinator and the Specialist(s) can often be stressful.

As mentioned earlier, the challenge for the servant-leader is to bring all the different orientations in line with each other in order to use the strong aspects of each side and reach convergences, without frustrating the individual team members. It is very important that he or she keeps the lines of communication open between the different disciplines, particularly because the biggest breakthroughs are often those made at the interface between border areas. Convincing the Specialists to stay attuned to other Specialists, and also to the people who want to make the product profitable, is critical. Furthermore, the Coordinator has to have the room to be able to adapt or shape the concept to the market, so that the final product can claim a worthy place in the company's offerings or product line.

It takes some creativity to be able to deal with the tensions between the Specialist's tunnel vision and the commercial motivation of the Coordinator. It is up to the servant-leader to get people to think beyond their old ideas and be open to the new ideas and input of their colleagues. When the Coordinator and the Specialists are able to succeed in joining forces with the intention of creating a new synthesis, the stage is set for breakthroughs. A nice example of this is NASA's space voyage to the moon, a project that required more than 100 technical specialists, and where the coordinator's role was obviously successfully filled.

However, if we assume that a Coordinator upsets the Specialists by threatening to *disregard* their *professional input*, then it is up to the servant-leader to reassure them by confirming that their professional skills are still needed and that they can contribute their individual expertise without having to give up anything.

Process of Consensus Versus Realization of Mature Product

The Teamworker Versus the Completer-Finisher

Still the work of the servant-leader is not finished. In the next phase of the innovation process there is a tension between the individual and the greater whole. Now that the different disciplines have worked together through the planning phase, it is time to get the endorsement of the whole group. The Plant, Monitor-Evaluator, Specialist, and Coordinator have begun the project, but if it is not completely finished or refined, no one will want to buy the product. To get the team on the same line, in both the technical and the social aspects, there is critical work to be done by the *Completer-Finisher* and the *Teamworker*. The Completer-Finisher is someone with an eye for detail that can make the whole system user-friendly. He or she has a keen sense for shortcomings and gaps and knows exactly if the team is on schedule. The Completer-Finisher makes sure that quality is guaranteed and that the product is delivered on time.

Team members are often less enamored with details and can become frustrated with the analytical and meticulous approach of the Completer-Finisher whose fear is that the next phase of the project will be squeezed for time. That is why the servant-leader brings in the Teamworker, the social-emotional specialist who preoccupies him- or herself with the "human factor." The Teamworker keeps the team's spirits high, acting as social glue by eliminating conflict points. He or she is kind and observant, which helps him or her to promote participation, facilitate team processes, and sometimes even repair fissures in the team. The best Teamworkers know when a team is incomplete and fill in the missing role. They understand what is going on under the surface and are often the first to sense that someone feels rejected or excluded, even if the person has not yet communicated this. Their skill contributes to lasting group cohesion.

The dilemmas that emerge in this phase are illustrated in Figure 7.3.

There is a tension that exists in the process of striving toward consensus *and* the development of a mature product. Endless discussion and consensus on every idea leads to "consensus for half-baked products" (1,10). Refining the embellishments can lead to losing sight of the actual use of the product—for example, "gold-plating flowers" (10,1).

The servant-leader chooses another way. You can't continue endlessly designing a new product, reconsidering characteristics or adding new aspects. This takes too long

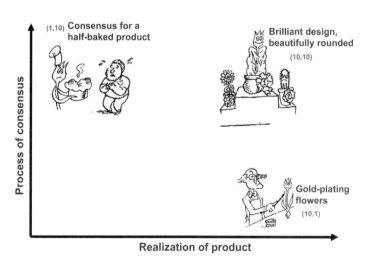

Figure 7.3 Process of consensus versus realization of mature product

and the focus of the product will be lost. On the other hand, you don't want to stop with your prototype too quickly just to put an end to the discussion. Who knows: that one last review to modify the existing model might improve it so much more. The result you strive for is a "brilliant design, beautifully rounded off" (10,10). In the end, what excites the client is a relevant, finalized product, not the harmonious process of consensus behind its completion.

Many people consider the process of refining a product or project as frivolous, but this is absolutely not the case. The servant-leader makes sure that the novelty is recognized by emphasizing all the more trusted aspects. He or she is the impresario or magnificent host of a fantastic show that convinces people to think that this is the new experience that they have been waiting for.

Conclusion

The Western economy operates on Adam Smith's principle of the invisible hand.[1] He argued that each individual, maximizing profit for himself, maximizes the total profit of society as a whole. Is there truth hidden in this adage? Absolutely. Does the society benefit when people, for selfish reasons of personal gain, try to better the service to the client? Certainly. Is this the only way to approach the dilemma? Definitely not! When it comes to cultural values there is not only one truth.

The reverse is also true. When teams and groups commit themselves to the larger whole, the individual members also profit from the "invisible hand." There are thus different "roads to Rome," and one is not better or more valid than the other. In some situations one approach might be better; in a different situation the other may be more effective. If you are adept at both approaches, you can use either at will.

In this specific dilemma different qualities and characteristics of the servant-leader play a role, which are closely related to the general concepts we dealt with in Chapter 1. The essential qualities of a servant-leader comprise the ability to facilitate a process that allows creative individuals to serve the team in order to jointly reach higher productivity. Conversely, the servant-leader can also ensure that the team feels and takes responsibility to serve the individual as the foundation of the whole. Naturally, in individualistic cultures the servant-leader will have the preference to begin with the creative individuals and encourage them to share the fruits of their endeavors for the collective. In more group-oriented cultures the servant-leader will rather spend that energy stimulating the team to encourage individual creativity. And thus, servant-leadership works in, and between, each and all cultures.

Resolution

Back to Peter Webber's reality: What should he do with the reward system at Cloverpill? How can he encourage the Moroccans, Americans, Japanese, and Dutch to work constructively together? One good option could be to give 50 percent of the variable reward to the individual, based on the contribution to the team as a team player. The other 50 percent could go to the teams that have successfully demonstrated their commitment to increasing individual creativity.

The reward system for the marketing staff and salespeople could be based on what the sellers have learned from their clients, as a form of co-opetition, much like in

> *the case of IBM and Shell, where individuals competed as to who worked the best with, first, their colleagues and then their clients. This is precisely what the servant-leader aims for.*

Notes

1   Adam Smith, *The Wealth of Nations* (London: Methuen & Co., 1904; first published 1776).

DILEMMA 4: CONTROL VERSUS PASSION

Challenge

Peter Webber has barely made it through the feat of dealing with the international reward system when he is confronted with the next dilemma. During the internationalization of the EMEA region the Germans and the Italians have come into conflict. Giovanni, the Italian general manager, wants an Italian colleague to fill a critical post, because he wants someone there with passion and vision. The Germans want to fill the position because they find that it is high time that they started making more profit. They are arguing for a German colleague who highly values control. Upon hearing this, Giovanni storms into Peter Webber's room and screams that this is the last thing that they need: an ice queen with the emotions of a robot. The German colleague retorts that he has seen too many spaghetti westerns here at Cloverpill already. Being a servant-leader, Peter Webber thinks, is not always easy.

The Dilemma

Is a servant-leader driven by passion or more by control? Since passion is only effective in the context of control, and control is only effective in a passionate context, the servant-leader needs to be able to integrate both. Obviously, being rational and expressing emotions are both important elements of functioning in life. For the servant-leader, which approach will be accented depends, in part, on which culture he or she comes from. People from a "neutral" culture place more value on the control of emotions in general, but they have moments and outlets for expressing emotions—for example, in Japan, during karaoke. In more "affective" cultures, where life is lived with passion, the servant-leader will have to look for more controlled processes.

In a neutral culture, it is generally accepted that openly showing your emotions is improper, though this does not mean that you are not allowed to have your emotions. It simply means that the measure to which you express your emotions publicly is limited. Neutral cultures accept feelings and are aware of them, but keep them under control. They interpret the loud and or exuberant signals of affective cultures as "over the top" or too emotional. In neutral cultures, being flamboyant or too expressive lowers a person's prestige. The fact that a Japanese business partner tends to limit his body language can make it more difficult for people from affective cultures to understand what he is thinking. Likewise, people from affective cultures often do not know how to pick up the subtler signs of neutral cultures. Such situations can lead to misunderstanding.

In an affective culture, people have no problem expressing their emotions. In such an environment, it is not necessary to hide your opinions or feelings. In fact, doing so is undesirable. Most people recognize that Italians, Spanish, Portuguese, and French are known to speak with their hands as well as their words to get their point across.

We need to be very careful when we generalize about these differences. People from neutral cultures are not cold and emotionless. The amount of emotions that are shown is often the result of situation and/or agreement. That said, even in a culture where people generally keep their emotions under strict control, strong emotions of pleasure or pain might show.

What is different is that cultures will share their emotions in varying degrees. The fury of the Frenchman whose car has been bumped and the manner in which he uses his body to show his anger is almost legendary. In stark contrast to this, it is almost forgivable if you think that your Japanese boss has fallen asleep during your presentation because he appears motionless. For those who do not realize that his way of sitting still with his eyes half-closed is a sign of respect, it could be quite irritating. Similarly, the long silences after a presentation can be unnerving for some, if interpreted as a sign of boredom, rather than a show of deep thought.

This specific dilemma is more nuanced and diverse than most of the others. This is because there is an ongoing discussion about which situations call for affective or controlled behavior. Despite their puritanical background, it appears that Americans are quite affective. They like to show their enthusiasm over products, visions, missions, and projects, but are less expressive in their relations with each other. They are OK about positive emotions, such as enthusiasm, but not about negative ones, such as anger and sadness. They talk about emotions (I am feeling anger) in a lightly therapeutic way, but they seldom show physical signs of anger.

The British often use humor to express their emotions and are known to start a speech with a joke to relax the crowd. Germans and the Swiss would see this as frivolous. The Japanese and Koreans will often show their wish for intimacy by going out drinking together. Generally Germans would rather keep their emotions to themselves, but will share their life philosophies. The patterns here are all extremely complex.

Double Focus

For a Chinese or northern European, a good leader will rarely show his or her emotions, raise his or her voice, or use extravagant body language. But for the Kuwaiti or Italian leader, showing emotions in these ways indicates a level of involvement. To ensure that these two very different cultures can work together, it is necessary that people do their best to learn how to interpret the other's signals and to moderate their own behavior.

Uncontrolled emotions lead to the perception of neurotic behavior, while a completely controlled person can come across as an automaton. Normally, both emotional and rational thinking are naturally more or less combined in some ratio. The servant-leader has both capacities within him or her and combines them. The emotions give depth to thought, and rational thought gains "life" by being tied to feelings. First rational thinking, and then emotions at the right moment to actualize the thought; or first feeling, and then pondering an effective way to share your feelings: both ways are examples of integration.

The Benchmark

In order to measure how open different cultures are to expressing their emotions, people from different countries were asked:

What is your opinion on the following remark?

In my society, it is considered unprofessional to express emotions overtly. In retrospect, I quite frequently think that I have given away too much in my enthusiasm.

The options to choose from ranged from "strongly agree" to "strongly disagree." An analysis of the answers is shown in Figure 8.1.

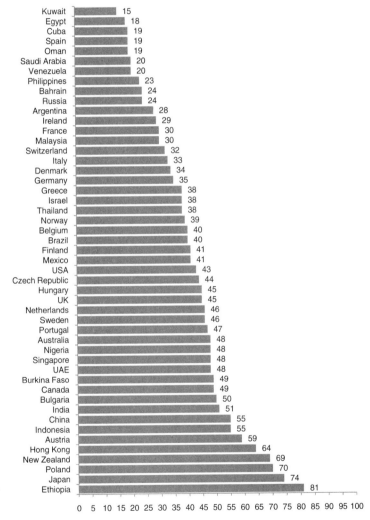

Figure 8.1 Controlled (neutral) versus passionate (affective) emotions. Percentage of respondents who tend not to show their emotions.

Problems and Solutions

The dilemma of passionate versus controlled emotions has to do with the legitimacy of expressing your feelings. This dimension is concerned with the measure to which your emotions are shown or controlled in the workplace. In this dilemma the following tensions play a role:

- Technical excellence versus aesthetic appeal
- Seriousness versus playfulness
- No-nonsense approach versus humor
- Controlled emotions versus passionate emotions

Technical Excellence Versus Aesthetic Appeal

Anders Knutsen, a servant-leader par excellence, was CEO of Bang & Olufsen from 1992 to 2001. The last big challenge he faced there was to guide his company through the looming crisis by making products that were both technically superior and aesthetically or emotionally appealing. This was a subtle and diffuse concept to master.

Fine audiovisual information needs to be transferred to instruments that are worthy of the artist and composition, just as the instruments of an orchestra attempt to re-create the emotions and the soul of the composer and transmit this to the audience.

Traditionally at Bang & Olufsen, technical excellence and emotional appeal were always important—more than sales or marketing—but these defining qualities were no longer in harmony. First, one had been dominant, and then the other, and the race to excel in both had priced the products out of the market. However, "Time is in our favor," Knutsen said. "The world is overrun with discount junk products that strive to become classics; products with an emotional value will be strongly placed in our 'throwaway' culture." [1]

In response to the situation, Knutsen initiated the "Idealand" concept at the end of the nineties, where, in a virtual space, engineers, music lovers, designers, and other people, both within R&D and outside the company, could discuss how to better integrate technique and aesthetics. As a result of this initiative, Bang & Olufsen's culture changed considerably, though the values remained the same, and they were increasingly able to strengthen each other. The secret of Bang & Olufsen's products—that each part in the system must work with every other part in the system—remains just as relevant and significant within the organization.

As a result, Bang & Olufsen tests its products with its clients, and when finalized, each one has an expected product cycle of ten years. "We position ourselves in a manner in the market that what is developed in Idealand will either be established or fail," says Knutsen. Idealand is not a private museum, but a test laboratory for viable ideas and, according to Anders Knutsen, allows the customer to answer "yes" or "no" to a set of hypotheses. This is the ultimate proof that a servant-leader connects passion with functionality.

Seriousness Versus Playfulness

Is a servant-leader a calm person who sometimes makes a joke, or is he or she someone who is always playful and from time to time makes a deep and insightful comment? Or, is it about something else? Is it about creating situations that can be described as "serious play"—for example, in business games? The purpose of business games is to communicate serious messages in a more fun and entertaining manner. Servant-leaders, who are concerned with making their organization a learning organization, often use this technique.

Learning is a serious process and education is a serious business. There is also another way of learning that is common in the business world and in daily life, which is learning by *trial and error.* When we make mistakes the first time round, we learn to quickly correct them. Getting to know your client, learning a language, trying to help or love someone, combining cultures to draw in foreigners, developing innovative activities: it is all a process of falling down and getting back up again.

But experiential learning is not merely undisciplined research on a "soft" subject. It is an important learning process for serious and complex questions in order to eliminate absolutely every mistake. To achieve this, mistakes are purposely created and corrected in models and simulations, after which the technique is ready for practice. World-class companies need to be able to play—serious games—if they really want to produce innovative products. Michael Schrage, author of *Serious Play*, advises, "When gifted innovators create, don't listen to what they technically describe but look at the models they make." [2] Whether it is a spreadsheet that tests a new financial product or a foam rubber prototype for a calculator, what interests Schrage is not the model itself, but the behavior that is inspired by it.

Schrage researches successful prototypes in companies such as AT&T, Boeing, Microsoft, and DaimlerChrysler. From this, he describes the sort of culture that favors innovation:

> *The essential message of* Serious Play *is that tomorrow's innovations will increasingly be the by-product of how companies and their customers*

behave—and misbehave—around this new gener-ation of models, prototypes, and simulations. The distinction between serious play and serious work dissolves as technology gives innovators ever-increasing opportunities to simulate and prototype their ideas.

Just as the methods of creating models are drastically chang-ing, so too will the organizations that use them.

According to Schrage, the ten rules of serious play are as follows:

1. Ask, "Who benefits?"
2. Decide what the main paybacks should be and measure them. Rigorously.
3. Fail early and often.
4. Manage a diversified prototype portfolio.
5. Commit to a migration path. Honor that commitment.
6. A prototype should be an invitation to play.
7. Create markets around the prototypes.
8. Encourage role-playing.
9. Determine the points of diminishing returns.
10. Record and review relentlessly and rigorously.

Playing happens where few costly mistakes can be made, in a simulated environment. Things get serious when the perfected technique is finally adapted to the actual situa-tion. As an extra precautionary measure, sometimes the technology can be self-cybernetic and self-correcting so that "Houston, we have a problem" can be immediately addressed. It is important to build in self-restoration or reboot possibilities.

To remain competitive, businesses often have to make decisions before all the facts have been collected. Thus, decisions have to be made on incomplete information, and therefore you can have situations that shortly after need to be corrected in situ. Harvard Business School's renowned "case learning" has been used for quite some time in British and North American law faculties. There is recognition, however, that every situation is unique and that precedence might only become clear after the judge or director has made a decision. Only then is it possible to see if the decision was good or bad.

Here, we again see how rational thinking is connected with the playful and the emotional. It is up to the servant-leader to lead this process.

No-Nonsense Approach Versus Humor

Is the servant-leader so controlled that he or she never cracks a smile, or is he or she always laughing, the joker who doesn't take things too seriously? Obviously, the answer is neither. You have servant-leaders who are controlled but at crucial moments know how to let loose. Other servant-leaders are more jovial, dealing with the world through laughter, but at crucial and unexpected moments know how to become very serious.

Comedy writers such as John Cleese ("Monty Python" and "Fawlty Towers"), John Sullivan ("Only Fools and Horses") and Matt Groening ("The Simpsons") are very different, but also very complementary. They all have one thing in common: the functional way they use humor. Just like Arthur Koestler, author of *The Act of Creation*,[3] they all believe that humor is closely connected with creativity. Why? Because humor is a process in which two "seemingly opposing logics" are actually both logical. This is what makes us laugh and this is of great importance for the servant-leader.

Koestler has shown that humor is based on *bi-sociation*, the mental and emotional ability to follow two split aspects of a thought process. This insight makes you laugh. Using bi-sociation through humor, managers can get a more complex overview of their organization. When they encounter contradictions, they use the notion of "and-and" rather than "either-or." Apparently, this orientation is impossible if we use linear thinking and a priori want to avoid mistakes. If we respect human diversity and different cultures, then the (business) world at once becomes full of dilemmas that we cannot solve with linear thought. An alternative, nonlinear approach is necessary to reconcile these dilemmas. Humor is one example of a powerful way to effectively deal with a dilemma.

Controlled Emotions Versus Passionate Emotions

There are some fantastic examples of leaders who are successful in intercultural groups because of the way that they can integrate control and passion. Take, for example, Richard Branson from Virgin. During a series of interviews THT did with different leaders, multiple microphones were needed to capture Branson's answers. He could not sit still; he was so passionate about the subjects at hand.

On the other hand, one microphone was more than enough for Michael Dell. Mr. Dell is tremendously self-contained—but you can feel the fire in the background, fueling him. The result was that when he did have a slight reaction, this gave his message more emphasis.

So what do these two servant-leaders have in common, besides that they have experienced international success?

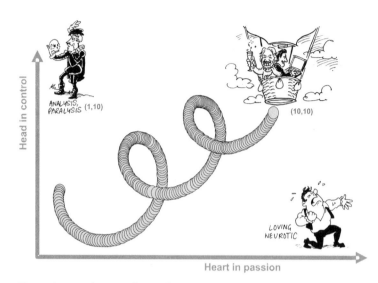

Figure 8.2 Head in control versus heart in passion

To name one trait, they both combine passion and thinking. Second, they both start from their strong points—for Dell, this is control and for Branson, this is emotion—and "check what your heart says." (See Figure 8.2.) They are the kind of leaders that Peter Webber should emulate.

Conclusion

The servant-leader cannot be characterized as a passionate person. On the other hand, he or she is not overly controlled and judicious either. The servant-leader not only unites both orientations in him- or herself but also helps others through the same process. Where the passionate Italian looks for moments to act rationally, the matter-of-fact English or Japanese look for moments where they can express their emotions. The Englishman often reaches for humor to legitimize emotions. The Japanese prefer to wait until after work to let their emotions show.

Resolution

How can Peter Webber help in choosing a leadership style that will be acceptable to the Italians and the Germans? The leadership style that works across cultures is one where the emotions are instilled in the context of seriousness and control and where there is also room for a light, relaxed approach. Conversely, this also means that a passionate group of people sometimes need to acknowledge the importance of a controlled presentation, which, though inspired by passion, should nonetheless be delivered in a sober style. One idea would be to give both a German and an Italian the responsibility for the function and to appoint a third person (neither German nor Italian) to act as a sounding board for issues concerning significant investment or innovation.

The servant-leader will try to give more meaning to his or her passion by expressing it in the context of control, and vice versa. In this way, both gain more meaning.

Notes

1   Fons Trompenaars and Charles Hampden-Turner, *21 Leaders for the 21st Century* (Oxford: Capstone Publishing, 2001), 144–146.
2   Michael Schrage, *Serious Play* (Boston: Harvard Business School Press; 1st edition, 1999).
3   Arthur Koestler, *The Act of Creation* (London: Pan Books, 1970).

DILEMMA 5:
SPECIFIC VERSUS DIFFUSE

Challenge

Peter Webber is in a monthly meeting to discuss the upcoming business issues with the EMEA country managers. The problem at hand is: continually increasing service costs.

What is interesting to note is that the southern European countries (primarily Italy, Spain, and France) are in agreement with their African and Middle-Eastern colleagues, in their mutual desire to invest more in services for the customer. The Dutch, English, and Scandinavian colleagues, on the other hand, emphasize the need to pay more attention to the costs. Let the customer explain, for once, why a whole series of antibiotics needs to be recalled on the basis of one upset stomach and some minor side effects, even though both Harvard and Cambridge have already stated that this is one of the best medicines that can be used.

And, once again, Peter Webber faces a situation that might more easily have been resolved if everyone had the same cultural background. But this is not the case, and moreover, it is about the expectations of the clients, which are also very different. So what should he do in a region like EMEA where these differences are making his job so complicated?

The Dilemma

In some cultures, a good leader is seen as the one who provides his or her organization with direction by means of specific tasks. This can lead to an emphasis or focus on shareholder value over and above other defined objectives. Other cultures have a preference for a leader who has a broader perspective and remains aware of social responsibilities, going for market share above profit.

In the first situation, we can talk about a "specific" culture. These cultures concentrate more on the individual parts. Focus is prioritized above context. In the second example, we speak of a "diffuse" culture, in which the reverse is true. The greater whole is of more importance, and context is more significant than focus.

People from specific cultures have a preference for dividing the whole into manageable parts in order to analyze them more easily. In these cultures, "the whole is truly the sum of its parts" and people feel most comfortable with "hard facts," numbers, standards, contracts, and other measurables. This need to narrowly define things in the work context also carries over into the private sphere, where every social activity is separate from other activities. The public space of a specific-oriented culture is much bigger then its private space. This means that, in the first instance, a newcomer is easily accepted, but afterward, it is much more difficult to move from someone's public space into the person's private sphere. The boundaries between work and private life are often well defined and protected. In specific cultures, people can easily conduct business without having first built up a relationship.

While specific cultures focus on quantity, diffuse cultures focus on quality. There is a notion that the separate

parts of a production process have an underlying intercon-
nection that is important. Making a good-quality product
requires joint responsibility. Through a general feeling of
involvement for the end product, a superior result can be
achieved at a lower cost.

People from diffuse cultures begin with the whole and
consider the different elements in a wider perspective. The
whole is thus *more* than the sum of its parts. Diffuse individuals have a larger private sphere and a smaller public
space. New people are not easily accepted in either area.
However, if they are accepted and invited into someone's
private sphere, then this usually counts for all layers of life.
A friend is a friend across the board. The different roles that
people play are no longer separated. Diffuse cultures nourish
quality of style, behavior, empathy, trust, and understanding. Developing a relationship is an absolute prerequisite for
doing business.

The dilemma here really revolves around the question
of what is the organization's essence: the technical/financial
dimension or the social/community dimension? Depending
on the culture, the balance could tip toward one side or the
other. Unilateral attention to the technical side can lead to a
climate of slavery, while focusing only on the social dimension runs the risk of degenerating into an unproductive social
club. A healthy company needs both. This is all the more
important because in an increasingly complex world things
that are independent are becoming an exception, so things
need to be viewed more in the light of their connection.

The servant-leaders know that they can only serve the
shareholders if they don't lose sight of the interests of the
society and the client. Reversed, they know that the society
continues to be served in a sustainable way as long as new
shareholder value continues to be created.

The Benchmark

There are many different ways to look at organizations, but which way best expresses the organization's true essence? In an effort to determine how people from different cultures think about this issue, people were asked to choose from the following two propositions:

> A: *An organization is a system designed to perform functions and tasks in an efficient way. People are hired to fulfill these functions with the help of machines and other equipment. They are paid for the tasks they perform.*
>
> B: *An organization is a group of people working together. The people have a social relationship with other people and with the organization. The functioning of the company depends on these relationships.*

It is obvious that answer A reflects a specific orientation, while answer B represents the diffuse perspective. Again, as is indicated in Figure 9.1, there is an enormous difference between different cultures in the way they answer the question.

Problems and Solutions

Some cultures have the tendency to analyze, reduce, and pick apart experiences into distinct parts, while others are more focused on creating a synthesis. The possible tensions between these two poles are endless and can contribute to the following conflicts:

- Text versus context
- Focus on the bottom line versus the development of people
- Shareholders versus society
- General public versus specialized group
- Work versus private life
- A "moment in time" versus the truth

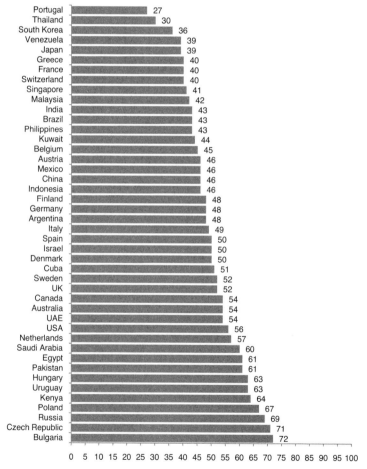

Figure 9.1 An organization is a "system" versus "a group of people." Percentage of people opting for answer A.

Text Versus Context

A number of years ago, Motorola introduced an interesting process called *Individual Dignity Entitlement* to stimulate dialogue between bosses and their subordinates. A couple of times per year, a discussion took place, revolving around six important questions such as: "Is the work that you do meaningful?" and "Do you have enough resources to do your job properly?" "Yes" and "no" were the only possible answers. If you answered "yes," there was no dialogue and you moved on to the next question. If you answered "no," a discussion ensued around what you needed in order to be in a state to answer "yes" next time.

This system, which had been launched by Motorola's CEO in Chicago, has worked fantastically in the United States, where transparency and measurability have a positive effect on motivation. When they applied the system to Korea they encountered something strange and unexpected. They could not explain why in this region 98 percent of the time people answered "yes," particularly as the local chip production was anything but successful!

After a number of interviews with the Koreans, it quickly became apparent that when faced with the system instigated by headquarters, although they appreciated the content, they had no idea how to deal with the American specificity. They had great difficulty making a choice between yes and no. In Korea, the answer to the boss is always yes, no matter what the question. Moreover, what was the reason for measuring and publishing this information?

An astute HR colleague in Chicago, who had a natural feel for servant-leadership, quickly spotted the difficulty. His suggestion was to slightly adapt the system for the Asians by removing the yes/no option and replacing it with a scale option. For those who pay close attention, a 90 percent "yes" on the scale is a subtle indication of a Korean "no."

Focus on the Bottom Line Versus the Development of People

The servant-leader is often caught between a world of delivering results to the shareholders and the need to develop employees. Kaplan and Norton's Balanced Scorecard [1] was designed to address this issue. The BSC management tool urges leaders to find a balance between the two cases. In practice, leaders often chose to focus on financial results one year and to develop their people the following year—and again make another choice the subsequent year. This drives away those employees who take learning and their career development seriously.

At one point, insurance giant AXA suffered from this kind of scenario. After five years of heavy cost reductions, a number of the better employees threw in the towel and went looking for companies that were willing to invest in people development. As a result, CEO Henri de Castres decided to increase the training budget by 25 percent. The only condition was that the service providers leading the training had to show how their interventions would affect the bottom line and increase profit.

This kind of solution is typical of a servant-leader. Servant-leaders look at how the greater objective of development can be used to achieve specific results as well as the other way around. Both approaches are valid. In the United States, they are more likely to first focus on results, and then use the extra profit to further train their people.

In Germany, they would rather take a different route: they would keep investing in their people, no matter what the circumstances, because they know this ultimately leads to better results. The development of their employees is a priority, even if it means that there is a lesser return for their shareholders. The difference in their vision is also reflected in their role as client. While the Americans will, after one bad quarter, pull back as client until things are looking positive again, the more diffuse Germans will remain loyal customers, even in the downturns. These are two very different approaches to the same dilemma.

Shareholders Versus Society

Many companies wrestle with the tension between shareholder value and their social responsibilities. How do you give authentic credence to social responsibility when you have shareholders breathing down your neck? Because, let's be honest, without the financial investors, there is less money to give away. It is a "chicken-and-egg" situation.

Servant-leaders take both responsibilities seriously. They appreciate that making money is "a must," in both the short and the long term. Thus, they will not become lazy, riding on the cushion of a cumulative profit of seven "fat" years, but will always be prepared to deal with the possible reality of seven "lean" years. The servant-leader will not obsess about the specific quarterly number. He or she knows all to well that the sustainability of the profit is dependent on society. At the same time, he or she also realizes that focusing only on the employees and the surrounding community is not enough. Ideals, nice as they are, do not in themselves generate money. The shareholders need a reasonable return on their investment if the company wants to be able to continue to fulfill its societal function. The thing about this is that if we take each extreme seriously and are able to integrate them, the end result is considerably better than either option alone.

A good example is Johnson & Johnson, which is one of the companies that Jim Collins looks at in his book *Good to Great*.[2] For decades, this company made abnormally high profits for its shareholders. Its returns were exceptionally striking considering that its credo, written as early as 1943, prioritizes shareholders last, after doctors, nurses, and patients, suppliers and distributors, management, the local and global community, and the environment.[3]

Our Credo

We believe our first responsibility is to the doctors, nurses, and patients, to mothers and fathers and all others who use our products and services . . .

Customers' orders must be serviced promptly and accurately. Our suppliers and distributors must have an opportunity to make a fair profit. We are responsible to our employees, the men and women who work with us throughout the world . . .

We must provide competent management, and their actions must be just and ethical. We are responsible to the communities in which we live and work and to the world community as well . . .

We must maintain in good order the property we are privileged to use, protecting the environment and natural resources . . .

Our final responsibility is to our stockholders. When we operate according to these principles, the stockholders should realize a fair return.

(Shortened and adapted version)

This is not because shareholders are not important for the company. If that were true, it would be difficult to explain why Johnson & Johnson belongs to the list of companies that pay out the most dividends, year after year. It is because Robert Wood Johnson, one of the founders and a servant-leader, linked the specific goals with the diffuse general societal responsibility, which began with patients, doctors, and nurses. Johnson & Johnson shows, unambiguously, that serving the society is the best guarantee of a sustainable profit for the shareholders. Societal responsibility rewards nicely.

General Public Versus Specialized Group

When Michael Dell started in the computer industry at the end of the last century, there were only two segments in the market: expensive, specialized computers and simple, inexpensive computers. He had to decide if he wanted to target a small, specialized group of users, or the general public. The choice was to offer high-quality products for a limited few or to reach a larger market with a uniform product. This is a dilemma that lots of leaders face. One route requires that you sacrifice profit, and the other asks you to sacrifice quality; neither is a choice that anyone can get really enthusiastic about. The risk of the first strategy is that the distribution channels clog up and there is no difference between your product and that of the competition. The second strategy also has risk in that the smaller niche markets limit the entrepreneur in their possibilities.

Dell did not let himself get caught in the limitations of this dichotomy and developed his own approach: the Direct Selling Model. The advantage of this model is not only the breadth but also the depth of the approach: the personal character and customized design. Dell broke with the con-

ventional wisdom that you must choose either a large customer base, or fewer customers with specialized, complex
problems and high service needs. His ability to bridge these
concepts establishes him as a servant-leader.

The connection he created was just as powerful as it
was simple. Through direct sales via one-on-one telephone
or Internet contact, he integrated breadth with depth and
complexity. The attraction of the Direct Selling Model via
the Internet is that you have a constantly growing number
of potential customers and that you can use the Internet to
give them directed information.

Work Versus Private Life

The servant-leader is attuned to the idea that one's work
is in harmony with one's private life. Leaders are often so
busy that they find it difficult to maintain their personal
lives, a reality supported by the fact that the divorce rate is
higher than average for this group. It seems that the specifics
of work take precedence over everything else that is called
"life." Servant-leaders will do all that they can to avoid falling into this trap; for example, by making sure that what
they strive to do is in tune with how they are at home. One of
the characteristics of servant-leaders is that their actions and
behavior are in line with "who" they are. In other words, they
do not act the part for someone else's benefit, but stay true
to themselves wherever they go. The beauty of this is that, in
the process, they are eliminating one source of stress.

It is often said that work and private life should be in
balance, but this is exactly not what the servant-leader strives
for. Balance is actually an example of a compromise and,
therefore, never the optimal solution. It is much like the idea
of having more time for your private life by answering half

your e-mails from home. Servant-leaders strive beyond the compromise to a real solution. In this case, the servant-leader is always looking for how to integrate work and life. That means that your work helps you to function better at home and a harmonious home life allows you to achieve a better performance at work. An example of this is "quality time," where you choose moments where you want to next focus.

A "Moment in Time" Versus the Truth

In Japanese restaurants the waiters and waitresses have a knack of appearing at just the right moment to ask if you would like some more sake or if the wasabi/soy sauce ratio is all right. It seems as if they are counting every sip, because their appearance is always remarkably timely. This style of service is in stark contrast with that of the Netherlands, where avoiding the eyes of the client at the crucial moments has all but become a national sport. If you get quality service, it is always for the things that you don't need. For some, the service in American stores is almost as irritating. The staff storm toward you as soon as you enter their store to ask how they can be of help, while you have not yet even had a chance to see what they have to offer.

Apparently it is an art to be able to offer something just at the right moment: "the moment of truth."[4] This expression was introduced by Jan Carlzon of SAS airlines. What he meant to express with it is that it is important for people in business to "go deep" at just the right moment. By properly assessing when it is important to "go the extra mile," you can exponentially increase your margins. Just exactly when this "right moment" is, is largely determined by culture.

The expectations around service standards are without doubt influenced by culture. Westerners are often shocked when they hear that an Asian bank has more than $2,000 billion outstanding in questionable loans. This is *real* service, and it is explainable: in these cultures, the client comes before all. If you, as a bank, have had a solvent client for years, you don't leave them in the dust at the first downturn! You have a diffuse relationship with them, and your relationship with them goes deeper than the financial connection. The dinners you shared in Tokyo leave you no choice. So you continue financing. The problem, however, is that this kind of relationship, in Japan, developed on a national scale. After ten years, the result was an ailing economy. This is in clear contrast with what the American business banks such as Lehman Brothers and Merrill Lynch have done for their clients. Only serving the short-term also has a downside, especially if you know that the interest rates are only going up. This is just asking for bankruptcy.

This compares drastically with what *soluble* Dutch banks offer: an enormous package of services that you can use, but only until the moment you actually need it. If you are shopping for a loan from a Dutch bank, the first question they will ask is, "What do you earn?" The second question will be, "What do you have in savings?" In other words, they only actually want to give you a loan if you already have money. Curious, is it not? The danger of the Japanese bank is service to the extreme without specific checks, while the Achilles' heel of the Dutch banks is the fact that it is easy to lose sight of the relationship with the client.

The cultural differences are nowhere as visible as in the airline industry. If you ask for breakfast on a North American short-haul, the likelihood is that you will be told, "Sorry, sir, but this flight is only ninety minutes, in which time we don't serve breakfast." At best, the flight attendant will bring you a basket with small bags of pretzels or chips and apologize that they don't serve peanuts. In contrast, if you fly with Cathay Pacific from Hong Kong to Taipei, during the fifty minutes of flight time you receive a warm breakfast that is actually so hot that it is difficult to finish it during the flight. This is a question of cultural differences. The specific American will argue that an airplane is not a restaurant. The diffuse Chinese sees the stomach and your comfort as part of the relationship. In a joint workshop with Cathay and American Airlines on the subject of "Serving the Client," someone came up with the idea to serve warm pretzels—brilliant, but not realistic, and also not really solving the dilemma.

The servant-leader's solution worked on the principle of the *moment of truth*. If you only ever focus on creating deep relationships with your client, you can quickly go bankrupt. It costs far too much time to always be at the beck and call of your customer. But if you never invest extra time in customers, they will walk away (to a competitor that is willing to go the extra mile) and you will also go broke. It is, therefore, in your interest to look at where the crucial moments are in your business where you can "mean more for your client" and make the connection between the part (moment) and the whole (truth).

Singapore Airlines, Southwest, and Virgin are examples of airlines that have taken a serious look at where their *moments of truth* lie. They know exactly which moments are the most important for their clients. That means that the clients get optimal service at the moments they most want or need it—if they miss their connection or lose their baggage, for example. Through the specific moment, a connection is made to the diffuse whole. Or, from the perspective of the servant-leader, the greater whole serves the specific moment and vice versa.

Naturally, here there are also preferences that are influenced by culture; for example, the specific American leader who first addresses your specific results and then rewards you with a long relationship with the organization along with sound career advancement. Jack Welch even went as far as asking 10 percent of his employees to find another job outside the company. However, employees who achieved specific results were deeply welcomed and integrated within the diffuse GE family. When working with the diffuse Japanese, the servant-leader starts with the diffuse father role from which the employees are addressed on their specific results. The dilemma is the same, but the starting point is different.

Conclusion

The servant-leader will not be dissuaded by the dilemma between technical/financial and social/societal. He or she is not interested in technical knowledge or social relations as such, but has his or her own more practical angle. For him or her, the issue is that people are productive. Servant-leaders who have a preference for a specific orientation would rather first focus on the specific aspects, such as profit and output. On this basis they develop their people. The more diffuse servant-leaders will begin with investing in their people. As a result of their acquired knowledge, these employees will contribute to the financial success of the organization.

Also, the dilemma is the same all over, but the solution is culturally predetermined. Specific cultures prefer to begin with a concrete point, with a (executive) summary, while diffuse cultures rather begin by building a context and there within find the solution. The servant-leader can, depending on personal preference, start on either side but will always keep making the connections. In this way, servant-leaders will continually test their concepts and ask themselves, "Does this work in practice?" From the work floor, though, they will also check the theory of what they are doing.

Resolution

Thus, what does this now mean for Peter Webber? The dilemma is clear. On the one hand, the diffuse cultures from Africa, the Middle East, and southern Europe want to build a sustainable and deep relationship with the customers and patients. On the other hand, the northern European cultures have a preference for a possibly shorter payment time for the client in order to satisfy the specific shareholders.

He will have to discuss with his team the "moments of truth" in the pharmaceutical industry. Just like Jan Carlzon of SAS, he will need to seek out what truly makes the difference in serving their clients. In the airlines, safety (which was taken for granted) and quality of food did not make a large difference. However, legroom, personal attention, and service when you miss a flight were considered very important. Market research that would determine what patients perceive as very important should be able to provide Peter Webber with the information needed for him to decide in which direction he should go in order to get the maximum return with a limited budget. And, just as in the airline business, these "moments of truth" will transcend the specific cultures. Always giving in to customers is just as unwise as neglecting them.

Notes

1   Robert Kaplan and David Norton, "The Balanced Scorecard: Measures That Drive Performance," *Harvard Business Review* (Boston: Harvard Business Review Press, 1992).

2   Jim Collins, *Good to Great: Why Some Companies Make the Leap . . . and Others Don't* (London: Random House, 2001).

3   Johnson & Johnson website (jnj.com).

4   Jan Carlzon, *Moments of Truth: New Strategies for Today's Customer-Driven Economy* (New York: Harper & Row, 1989).

DILEMMA 6: SHORT TERM VERSUS LONG TERM

Challenge

"Here come the English again, with their sole focus on shareholder value." Peter Webber sighs. "When I make a plan for the next three years, it always gets criticized by the short-term thinkers. Sure," he snorts, "shareholder value . . . for the people who never share." Thankfully, in this case, the French are backing him. They think his marketing plan for the next three years is worthwhile, even if it means a bit less profit in the coming period. They feel that the payback will far outweigh the investment in the short term.

Furthermore, from the perspective of creating synergies in marketing, the French are willing to work on a number of projects simultaneously, but the English and German representatives are dead-set against the idea. They prefer a step-by-step approach—"All this hodgepodge ratatouille of the French is nice with a little garlic, but in business it is not direct enough." The differences between his team leaders' time horizons are making Peter Webber's life difficult. Should he go for the short or long term? He decides to sleep on it one more night.

The decision is judicious because "sleeping on it" is nothing more than letting your subconscious speak; the decision has already been made, but we can't see it yet.

The Dilemma

The servant-leader has a good sense of timing: more than just visionary. Such a leader also has respect for tradition, a respect from which decisions are taken in the interest of the future. Furthermore, he or she can respond quickly and adequately to the environment but also knows when to take a step back in order to make the right decision. Finally, the servant-leader connects the short and the long term, daily operations with the corporate vision.

The way that people deal with time differs substantially by culture. This is difficult for business because activities need to be coordinated. Leaders have to deal with the varying expectations regarding time.

Time has several different aspects: to begin with, the relative importance placed on the past, present, and future (A). Second, there are various ways in which cultures structure time. Some cultures have a linear notion of time, in which time is seen as a series of sequential events and in which there is a preference to do one thing at a time, and there are cultures with synchronic notions of time, where the different events can take place at the same time (B). Finally, there are some cultures with a preference for a short time horizon and other cultures with a preference for a long time horizon (C).

We will zoom in on all three of these aspects below.

(A) Relative Importance of the Past, Present, and Future

The first difference we will look at concerns the relative importance people bestow on the past, present, and future. Saint Augustine stated in his *Confessions* that time, as a subjective phenomenon, can differ from time as an abstract concept. In its abstract form we cannot know the future because it is not there yet, and the past can be even less known. We have memories—partial and selected—but the past is no longer. The only thing that exists is the present, our only entry to the past or future. Saint Augustine wrote: "The present has three dimensions: the present of past things, the present of current things, and the present of future things." [1] Depending on where the accent is, we can distinguish three kinds of culture orientations:

1 Past-Oriented Cultures

If a culture is primarily oriented on the past, then the future is seen as a repetition of earlier experiences. Respect for older generations and for collective, historical experiences is characteristic of such a culture. In the business world, financial people tend to be partial to the past.

2 Present-Oriented Cultures

A culture that is mainly focused on the present will place relatively little value on experiences of the past or on future plans. Instead, daily experience determines thoughts and actions. For example, you will find that sales staff often have a short-term orientation, based on the "here and now." For them, it is all about getting a signature on the dotted line and clinching the deal.

3 Future-Oriented Cultures

As the name says, in a future-oriented culture, most of the activities are primarily determined by future prospects. When people are "charting a course" for the future, the past does not play an important role. Discussions regarding detailed planning, however, are very common. Within companies, the people working on business strategy are often future oriented.

(B) Sequential Versus Synchronic Notions of Time

With regard to structuring time, there are two approaches: sequential (linear) time and synchronic (parallel) time.

Sequential (linear)

For people who have a linear thinking process, time ticks by in an unwavering line, second after second, hour upon hour. For them, time is as an empirical given, a bound concept of successive segments. People who think sequentially tend to do one thing at a time. They are wild about planning and do their best to ensure the plans are followed. For them, coming to a meeting on time is "a must."

This linear notion of time led to Newton's idea of the universe as a "big clock." Although the idea has since been debunked, it played an enormous role in scientific history. Moreover, the framework it provided functioned as a life buoy, providing people something to hold on to in the midst of chaotic reality.

However, the danger in cultures where people talk about a constant "race against the clock" is that they can't keep up with themselves. It has been shown that those who are "governed by the clock" display more signs of mental instability and stress. The linear notion of time also accounts for an overestimation of logic. Also, the attempt to shield oneself from existential uncertainty, by measuring the world, works against the creative powers of the universe. Linear logic leads to "cause and effect" thinking that allows little room for creative synthesis, lateral thinking, diffuse processes, spontaneous inter-actions, system thinking, and other synchronic phenomena. Another problem of the linear notion of time is that it has a ten-dency to detach people from the "here and now." In an attempt to get the most out of life before our time here on Earth is up, we sometimes let the really important moments of life go by.

Synchronic (parallel)
In the synchronic approach, time is a cycle given in min-utes, days, weeks, months, and years. For people in such cultures, time is an extendable notion that allows them to do many things at the same time. In their view, time is a flex-ible given. Engagements have the characteristics of a good intention rather than an absolute appointment, and plans are easily changed. Although some people might come later to a meeting, it is probable that they gave the prior meeting their time and attention, and it can be expected that they will also stay and give the same attention to your meeting, regardless of scheduled ending times.

While linear people can barely do one thing at a time, synchronically programmed people can do a lot of things at the same time. It has been said that women are better at this than men. Rather than "a race against the clock," people from these cultures see life more like a dance. Here the trick is to dance in rhythm with the environment.

In Japan, the synchronic notion of time has made indus-trial adjustment: the *just-in-time* delivery of the stocks and the *split-second* coordination of the activities in the factory. Here stockpiles are not meters high. Staff know both what is needed and, right down to the split second, when it is needed, and that reduces costs. The flip side of the coin is that the synchronic notion of time is not always effective.

When important activities need to be planned on "favorable days," possibilities for production become more limited. In this respect, you need a lot of patience.

People in linear cultures often feel overwhelmed when they have to deal with a barrage of people in an unstructured way. The tendency for people in crowded spaces to not form a line but to all simply press forward together can, for people who are not used to it, feel like an invasion of their personal space. Perhaps the thing that annoys the sequentially (linearly) oriented Americans and northern Europeans the most is the synchronic (parallel) tendency of people to make, in their minds, inappropriate claims on their time—for example, by being late for appointments.

The way in which people in different cultures structure time has consequences for business practices. Take a simple, everyday example of buying food in the delicatessen. In countries with a sequential time orientation, such as in the United States, Great Britain, or the Netherlands, you might figuratively or literally "take a number" when you walk into the store, which tells you your place in the line. The person behind the counter helps each person in the order of arrival before he or she moves on to the next one. This is an efficient system.

It is not, however, the only system that works. The process can happen completely differently. Take for example the delicatessen in Italy, where if you ask the shop's butcher for salami, there is a good chance that he will call through the store, "Anyone else here who wants salami?" and in one action will take care of all the salami orders for the remaining customers on the premises. This is also an efficient system. The salami has to be unwrapped only once and the knife cleaned only once as well. Moreover, this process promotes a social interaction between the clients who have something in common—in this case, the desire for salami.

(C) Time Horizon

There are significant differences between cultures when it comes to how far people look forward and backward. Some cultures need to look years ahead to be able to survive. The long Swedish time horizon can be attributed to the country's long winters. In the short summers, everything for the rest of the year has to be planned. Also, for centuries, they have lived off the export of timber, so they know all too well that it will take another thirty-five years before they will have a sizable tree to replace the one they just chopped down. At the other extreme you have the Ethiopians and Iraqis who are so proud of their heritage that they often look backward into the past.

Our time horizon also shapes the way we do business. The long-term horizon of the Japanese can be sharply compared with the "quarterly thinking" of the Americans. This difference in perspectives was nicely illustrated when Japanese Matsushito tried to buy the operations at Yosemite National Park in California. The Japanese started with presenting a 250-year business plan. You can just imagine the reaction of the Californian authorities: "Yikes, this means 1,000 quarterly reports."

The tension between the short and the long term is also palpable between functional cultures, such as R&D and marketing. R&D staff can complain until they are blue in the face that marketers give them barely enough time to produce an adequate piece of work. Marketing does not often allow much time to produce, test, and refine a product. In these situations, most of the profit is lost when workers are enhancing the product according to the originally expected specifications. Marketers, for their part, complain about the lack of flexibility and the reaction time of the researchers.

The Benchmark

Tom Cottle's Circles Test was used to measure how people think about time in diverse cultures.[2] The test asks respondents to draw three circles that represent the past, present, and future. They are free to determine the size of the circles and place them in relation to each other as they wish. While the size of each circle says something about the importance of the past, present, and future, the positioning of each on the page provides insight as to the relationship between the three. (See Figure 10.1.)

The combination of numbers with the following statements makes it possible to determine if a culture has a preference for a sequential (linear) or synchronic (parallel) time structure.

Give a number, 1, 2, 3, 4, 5, 6, or 7, for each beginning and end of a time zone, where:

   7 = Years

   6 = Months

   5 = Weeks

   4 = Days

   3 = Hours

   2 = Minutes

   1 = Seconds

My past begins _____ from now

and ends _____ from now.

My present begins _____ from now

and ends _____ from now.

My future begins _____ from now

and ends _____ from now.

Past, Present, and Future

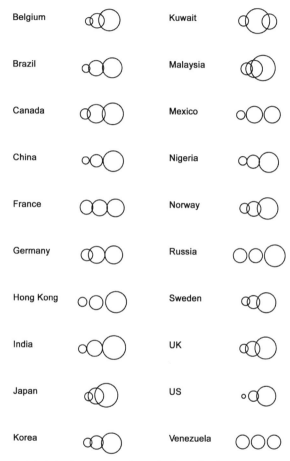

Figure 10.1 Relative importance of—and relationship between—past, present, and future. (The circle on the left represents the past, the circle in the middle represents the present, and the circle on the right represents the future.)

These statements give insight into the overlap between time horizons, or, in other words, their level of synchronism. The correlations were high and significant when compared to the overlap of circles. Research into the time horizon differences between R&D and marketing as functional groups, for example, showed that the time horizons of those in marketing were clearly shorter than those working in R&D.

Figure 10.2 illustrates some of the scores, per functional group.

Problems and Solutions

The time-related dimensions have to do with the manner in which people experience the passing of time: chronologically or in recurring patterns, as well as whether something is of a short or long duration. As a result of these orientations, the following tensions can arise:

- Past, present versus future
- "Hare brain" versus "tortoise mind"
- Command and control versus delegated autonomy
- Successive versus parallel

Past, Present Versus Future

Should servant-leaders preoccupy themselves with leading their colleagues to a richer and brighter future or do they serve them better by having respect for the past? The answer is, clearly, the servant-leader does both. This was certainly the case for a manager of a Dutch company in Ethiopia who was considerably frustrated by the planning of a workshop on change management, organized for, and with, Ethiopian managers. No matter what issue was discussed, the Ethiopians had the constant desire to return to the far past of their history. Development principles that

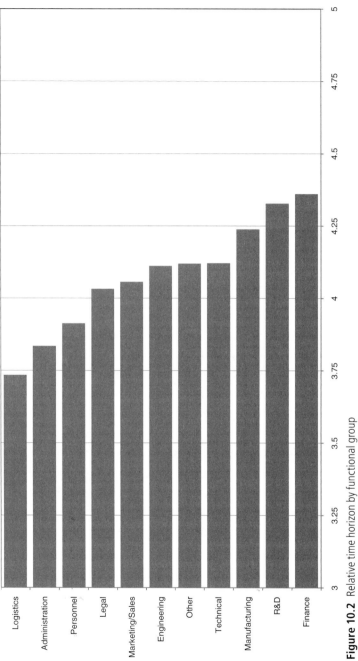

Figure 10.2 Relative time horizon by functional group

were not based on successful practices in the country's past did not stand a chance.

Finally, the manager was advised to look into the Ethiopian history texts and to read them from the perspective of modern management. What were the principles that had previously contributed to the flourishing trading life that Ethiopia had once known long ago? He was also told to examine the business reports of the company, which had a rich history within Ethiopia. These were conscientiously studied.

Armed with this knowledge, the Dutch leader dived into his work again, this time from a new perspective. He now positioned the future as the way to revive the great momentum of the past. He immediately received enthusiastic support from the management. Never before had this culture, which was oriented toward the past, invested so much energy in creating a prospective future.

A servant-leader will always attempt to connect the past, present, and future in such a way that the element that is most important in that particular culture can be used as the source of inspiration. In a country such as France, you see that the future becomes interesting when you have the possibility of "making history." This explains why the French are so avant-garde. Prestigious modern projects such as the Eiffel Tower, the French National Library, and La Défense will one day become a part of ancient history.

But the servant-leader that comes out of a future-oriented culture will do the opposite. In this way, servant-leaders such as Bob Galvin of Motorola, William C. Weldon of Johnson & Johnson, and Jeroen van de Veer of Shell regularly refer to the rich history of their organization, which is anchored in their company values and principles. Sometimes this even happens when the connection between history and business principles is not so strong.

"Hare Brain" Versus "Tortoise Mind"

Is the servant-leader a "Speedy Gonzalez" type, rushing from place to place, or a more thoughtful person who takes his or her time? In other words, is he or she more about quick solutions or thoughtful reflection? Or is this the wrong question? Of course, the organization is best served by both. Guy Claxton, author of the bestseller *Hare Brain, Tortoise Mind: Why Intelligence Increases When You Think Less*, makes a fundamental distinction between "hare brain" and "tortoise mind."[3] The hare brain is logical, quick, analytic, and good at mechanistic thinking. As described in the fable, the tortoise is slower, less focused, receptive, and more playful, almost a dreamer. The tortoise uses what Claxton calls the "undermind"—a kind of intuition. The undermind blossoms through rest and meditation. When a creative solution is needed, or if a problem is not yet clearly defined, the tortoise mind, with its thoughtful and meditative qualities, offers outcomes.

With our hare brains we could quickly come to the conclusion that creativity is born in the tortoise mind. Undoubtedly, the tortoise mind makes a difference. Reflect for a moment: Under which circumstances have your best ideas appeared? When did they happen? Let's guess, you were probably more or less relaxed and certainly not stressed about needing to come up with a breakthrough solution. However, you were also not sitting quietly, just waiting for the ideas to bubble up by themselves. Perhaps it was during a vacation, or under the shower, or simply in a moment of relaxation when you last had a number of ideas pop into your head, about how to tackle that difficult project.

So, what characterizes servant-leaders in this regard? Should they take some distance or energetically throw themselves at their work? Indeed—you guessed it—the two sides need each other in order to get beyond just having ideas, to having *really good* ideas. The servant-leader will always take care that the hare brain and the tortoise mind continue to work together. The road to effectiveness and creativity passes through hard work. First, it is important to think with the hare brain; then let the ideas rest and think them over quietly (tortoise mind) in order to, in the end, evaluate logically and systematically (again the hare brain). In this way, an upwardly circling spiral is created.

People seem to be happier about their decisions if they don't think about them so much in the beginning. If we go back to the title of Claxton's book, in this sense it is true that people that think less are more intelligent.

Command and Control Versus Delegated Autonomy

It goes without saying that leaders delegate authority, but for how long should they give their employees freedom before they reassert their control? Parents treat their two- or three-year-old children differently from how they treat their fifteen-year-old. Is this sensible? Of course it is! Servant-leaders have the same approach.

The Canadian psychiatrist Elliot Jaques was the first one to look at time orientations as an important element of leadership.[4] Good leaders can be recognized by their long "time span of discretion," which means that they have a sense of responsibility for their decisions far into the future, even if they might not officially be a part of that future.

Jaques discovered that generals from the Pentagon still felt some level of responsibility for the next ten to twenty years, even if they were obliged to retire early. That is an important finding. Investing in technologies that are essential for the future requires a lot of patience. Great leaders stand at the helm for decades, charting a course on long-term goals. As a manager, you can make an investment of one million euros in a refinery that will only be written off in thirty years, while you might be in a different functional position within three years (as was not uncommon at Shell). However, this does not release you from your responsibilities for the full thirty years of your decision! In order to cultivate this sense of responsibility, Shell initiated a practice of letting people change jobs every three years, though within the context of a lifelong career with the company. Jaques could see the leadership potential in young people by observing how far into the future they foresaw their planning and actions.

Another aspect of servant-leadership is related to the question of how long people give others freedom to do their work independently before there is a question of control. Some control from up above is necessary, because leaders are ultimately evaluated on the results. However, servant-leaders distinguish themselves in this process by the large amount of freedom and responsibility they give to their workers. In dilemma terms, it is a simple contrast between responsibility on the vertical axis and autonomy on the horizontal axis, as depicted in Figure 10.3.

The amount of autonomy depends upon the distance between the rotations of the spiral, since every time the spiral soars up, the manager is "controlled." Every time the spiral swings to the right, another episode of "autonomy" begins. Servant-leadership depends on how much autonomy is granted to those who report to the leaders. They are "free" inside of their "time-spans of discretion."

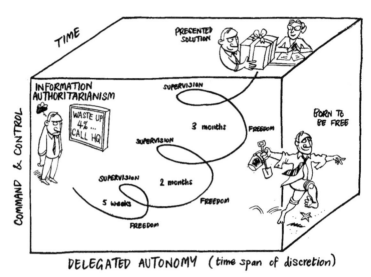

Figure 10.3 Command and control versus delegated autonomy

Successive Versus Parallel

There is scarcely a more competitive industry to be found than that of the automobile industry. The game here has been played on the cutting edge for decades. The suppliers, the dealers, and the clients all know this. Thus, there is a lot to learn from this game. Many management principles and solutions have sprung out of this industry, including the practice of integrating successive and parallel thinking—also an attribute of the servant-leader. This has to do with the need to bridge many opposing values, starting with the concept of the car itself.

A car needs to go *fast*, but it also has to be *safe*. Moreover, a car needs to be *compact*, but it also needs to have the maximum amount of *space*. It should be *inexpensive*, and *comfortable*. If you think about it, it is amazing how they are able, for the price of a Volkswagen in 1970 (after inflation correction), to have a car that not only is elegant but also has the latest technical gadgets on board. Finally, the driver must have the idea that he or she has the car *under control*, by using the *control equipment* that the car has installed.

The insights gleaned from the auto industry resulted in the birth of the *mass-customization* process, a successful combination between mass production and satisfying special client requests on a large scale. By standardizing certain parts, such as the chassis, motor, and underbody, it is easier to tailor the upper body to the color and wishes of the client or customer. Ford has been able to hoist both a Volvo and a Jaguar on a similar platform, thereby making huge quality improvements while at the same time lowering costs. Both Volvo and Jaguar have, in turn, been able to retain their identity by using nonvisible, standardized parts. The financial sector could learn an awful lot from this.

Also, in the area of production processes, the automobile industry has had an influence on other branches. "Just-in-time" production, which we referred to earlier, came out of Japan, where they were able to unite the sequential in production with the need for synchronic, or parallel, processing. At just the right moment, the speed of the sequence can be increased if, at that very moment, the different inputs are synchronized. The servant-leader knows this all too well. The best way to speed up the sequence line is to synchronize it "just in time."

Conclusion

For the servant-leaders, there are no barriers that are insurmountable. They are constantly in a state of development, with no end to their learning. There are dilemmas, naturally, and they differ according to the industry or the culture. However, with enough skills and power, the servant-leader can keep developing creative solutions.

The past several years have seen significant threats to the business world and to the learning organization, such as the credit crisis; from the Dutch side, the crises of Ahold and Shell are examples, not to mention Enron and WorldCom. In the light of these affairs, servant-leaders ask relevant questions. Do we go for short-term or long-term sustainability? Do we tackle everything at once, or piece by piece? And how do we change the future if the most important orientation is the past? These are all contrasting options that keep the servant-leader up at night but that he or she can solve with creative thinking. How? By not falling into the trap of tunnel vision or leaning to either side, but by combining the best aspects of the different notions of time.

In this way, the synchronic and short-term-thinking French servant-leader will develop an "emerging" strategy by trial and error. But because he or she does this in the framework of a vision, the long term serves the short. The sequentially and long-term-oriented Swede prefers to think about the long-term consequences as a "grand strategy," in which he or she takes short-term actions. Here the short term serves the long. Mintzberg calls both approaches "crafting strategy."

Resolution

Back to Peter Webber's problem. To begin with, we advise Peter to do his best to gather as many ideas and as much experience as he can and then to "sleep on it" for a night or two. After, he will need to put the French at ease by promoting the long term, while with the English, Italians, French, and Germans he will need to discuss the separate steps that are necessary to trace out the path to that future.

It all appears so easy if you are a servant-leader.

Notes

1   Augustinus, *Confessions* (Oxford: Clarendon Press, 1992).
2   Tom Cottle, "The Circles Test: An Investigation of Perception of Temporal Relatedness and Dominance," *Journal of Projective Technique and Personality Assessment*, No. 31, 1967.
3   Guy Claxton, *Hare Brain, Tortoise Mind: Why Intelligence Increases When You Think Less* (USA: HarperPerennial, 1999).
4   Elliot Jaques, *A General Theory of Bureaucracy* (London: 1976).
5   Henry Mintzberg, "Crafting Strategy," *Harvard Business Review* (Boston: Harvard Business Review Press, July 1987).

DILEMMA 7:
PUSH VERSUS PULL

Challenge

Peter Webber is satisfied. It was nice speaking with the marketing people. The meeting provided quite a few new insights, including knowing that the creativity of these people is indispensable to Cloverpill's success. Nevertheless, he has been placed in an almost impossible dilemma. Ever since the meeting he has been struggling with whether he should continue creating products and educating the markets, as they have always done in the United States and northwest Europe, or whether he should actually listen more to the existing needs of the clients, the patients.

Both have their pros and cons. Cloverpill has a reputation to maintain as a company that always brings the latest products to the market. But the African and Indian practice of using the clients' needs as a starting point is also worth taking into consideration. With this goal in mind, he has even invested in new SAP software. This system will help to connect diverse business processes. The margins might be lower, but India and Africa are enormous markets.

This gives rise to an essential question: Does Cloverpill want to be known as a market leader, or as a follower of client needs? The servant-leadership of Peter Webber is being tested once again.

The Dilemma

Westerners are generally raised with the notion that they should take destiny into their own hands and prevent unanticipated events. A leader is often respected when he or she is strong, bold, and outspoken. "Be assertive!" "Be brave!" "Have courage!" These are expressions commonly heard. In other parts of the world, a leader is more often someone with emphatic capabilities, someone who can imagine how it is to stand in the other's shoes. Therefore, listening skills are more developed than talking skills. Modesty is one of the more common characteristics. Precaution is valued more than bravado.

A servant-leader realizes that both viewpoints have their pluses. Connecting willpower with modesty, internal with external, and push with pull will ultimately lead to the greatest effectiveness.

This dimension revolves around a relationship with nature and the environment that we live in. Each culture develops an attitude toward its natural surroundings; the way people treat their habitat—internal or external—is strongly related to the way in which one tries to control life and fate. There are two basic attitudes: survival by adapting or by fighting.

In cultures that thrive on "internal control" (push), virtue is regarded as something that is within each person. The soul, the will, convocations, and principles are what inform one's thinking and ways of acting and are at the core of one's identity. In such cultures, people thus work from their inner strengths using their personal power. Here, "talking" comes before "listening," courage comes before caution, and willpower before modesty. Fate and luck do not exist; thus, there is an admiration of courage, control, and the expression of willpower. As personal judgment is the ultimate tool for measuring action, there is much appreciation for people who express their personal moral messages with all their heart. The idea that virtue is given by birth and thereby an important guiding principle is typical in Judeo-Christian cultures. In fact, it is this conviction that underpins Martin Luther's famous saying: "Here I stand; I can do no other."

In cultures that are externally controlled, that message would not be perceived in the same way. Here, people are led by what comes to them from their environment. They believe that you can never entirely control something, and they are, therefore, more flexible and cautious by nature. They are keen listeners and come across as quite modest. First they listen, and only then they talk. The starting point is cautiousness; only from there are risks taken. Thus, modesty is favored above willpower. In such cultures, virtue is perceived as something that is outside oneself, which one can draw strength from. It lies within things like natural rhythms, the overwhelming power of nature, beauty, and relations. These things serve as a source of inspiration for one's actions. From this perspective, the essence of virtue is to be flexible and adaptive to social and natural powers.

Double Focus

The crucial questions in this dilemma are as follows: What drives people? Are they internally motivated and, as such, operate from the inside out? Or does the inspiration for their behavior and choices come to them from their environment? In reality, both happen. Everyone has an inner compass that guides him or her. As the examples described later in this section will clearly confirm, a complete internal orientation leads to recklessness and ignoring external signals. This absence of feedback makes one careless, which can have disastrous results. The reverse attitude is also not desirable. A total external orientation and pure trusting in fate do not lead to taking action. By connecting these two points of view, optimal results are reached. The servant-leader does just that: connecting the inner with the outer, courage with caution, and push with pull.

The Benchmark

In order to measure whether cultures are mainly internally or externally driven, people were asked to respond to the following statements:

> A: *What happens to me is my own doing.*

In order to measure the value for typical external factors such as fate, luck and coincidence, the following proposition was put forward:

> B: *Sometimes I feel that I do not have enough control over the directions my life is taking.*

There was a clear difference between the cultural responses, as evidenced in Figure 11.1.

Problems and Solutions

This last dimension is actually about "locus of control." Is this point within us or outside—in our environment? Said in another way, are we the captains of our own ship, sailing our own course, or do we follow the winds of the sea? Here, the following tensions can arise:

- Courage versus caution
- Push versus pull
- Internal business perspective versus client perspective
- Taking charge versus adaptation
- Willpower versus discretion

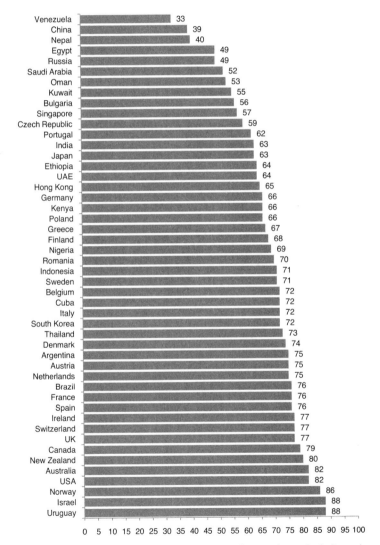

Figure 11.1 Captains of our own fate. Percentage of respondents who believe what happens to them is their own fate.

Courage Versus Caution

In the literature on servant-leadership, an image arises of the leader as someone who, through his or her courage and visionary capabilities, achieves remarkable results. The truth is often otherwise.

If a marketing manager puts forward a groundbreaking—but risky—plan at a board meeting and the CFO's reaction is, "be cautious," then the servant-CEO has to act. Courage isn't everything. Companies like the Dutch Ahold, the Belgian-Dutch Fortis, and the French Vivendi were led almost to the abyss by their (over)confident leaders. In politics, we know President Bush as a man of courage. What do these men have in common? Indeed, they do not see their courage in a context of caution.

But being too cautious is also not the answer. Companies such as Cable & Wireless and Unilever have not, thanks to their overly cautious leaders, always reached the desired results. In politics, the same can be said of President Mitterrand and Chancellor Schroeder. That is what happens if cautiousness is not placed in the context of courage.

A servant-leader should not be seduced into making a choice between daring and caution—"either-or"; he or she neither does a bit of both—"and-and." What he or she *does* do is to fully integrate both sides—"through-through."

Decisions that are made in this way are enriching and successful because they build on each other. In other words, they have integrity, defined as "creating a whole by integrating opposites." The servant-leader searches for solutions that are characterized by combining a high level of risk with a high level of security. However, devaluation occurs when these two values frustrate each other. The first tension produces a "virtuous circle" while the second produces a "vicious circle."

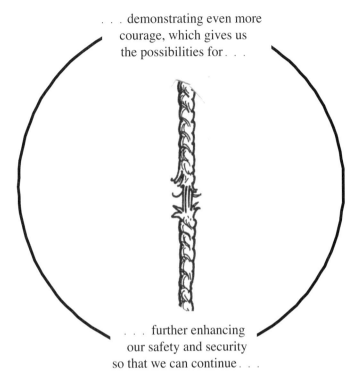

. . . demonstrating even more
courage, which gives us
the possibilities for . . .

. . . further enhancing
our safety and security
so that we can continue . . .

Figure 11.2 Virtuous circle

In Figure 11.2, you see that, in a virtuous circle, both risk taking and building in security can work well together. More importantly, this kind of approach generates synergies. There is a creative tension on the rope that holds both sides together. While illustrated as a circle, this process actually works as a spiral: by building in safety nets, it is easier to be more courageous, and, with this courage, you can take the necessary risks to try new ideas and improve safety even further.

In the vicious circle (Figure 11.3), the values are diametrically opposed. The cord that represents the tension between them is broken, all reservation and moderation

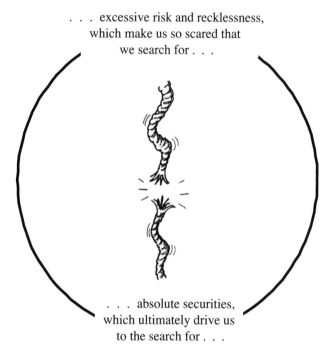

Figure 11.3 Vicious circle

destroyed. The system swings from reckless risk taking to panicky protectionism, back to recklessness, and so on, because the two opposite values exacerbate each other when positioned as enemies. In this negative spiral, the system will ultimately destroy itself.

The values are both absolute in one sense and related in another sense. The servant-leaders are healthier, richer, and wiser if they can combine both meanings. Risk taking and caution are both absolutely necessary for achieving well-being and prosperity. Unfortunately, there is no standard formula for combining the two elements. Servant-leaders take up the challenge to find, in ever-changing environments, the optimal synthesis.

What the optimal synthesis is, is largely culturally dependent. American and northwestern Europeans seem to have a preference for courageous leaders, while Latin American and Asian cultures tend to start from a position of caution. Caution forms the basis from which courage can be demonstrated: the same dilemma, with different starting points.

Push Versus Pull

Another core quality of today's servant-leaders is their capability to integrate market feedback into technology that was developed by the company and vice versa. A choice between "technology push" and "market pull" is not very fruitful. The leader knows that a technology push will ultimately lead to a dead-end niche (that part of the market without any consumers). On the other hand, an exclusive focus on the market will leave the company at the mercy of clients. The solution, again, lies in making a connection.

In the business world, there is more and more talk about added values. But does this work in light of this particular dilemma? Servant-leaders do not add values; they combine them: fast *and* safe cars, good *and* easy-to-make food. No one is suggesting that combining values is easy, but it is possible. A computer that makes complex calculations can also be user-friendly—it only takes creativity and the capacity to let go of certain thinking patterns. Indeed, the most complex value systems form the context in which international leadership can show its merit.

To illustrate this, take Dutch electronic giant Philips as an example. This company faced two different dilemmas of innovation. To start with, there was an obvious tension between the push of technology and the pull of the market.

The key question was: What do we do? Do we make something we can and want to make, but for which there is not yet a market? Or do we take the requests and wishes of the client as a starting point and feed this into our R&D and product planning functions? Neither of the extreme focuses leads to a sustainable innovation.

In the past, the pure "push of technology" had worked in the internally controlled societies of Great Britain, the Netherlands, and the United States. A purely client-driven focus, on the other side, had worked well in externally oriented cultures such as Japan and other Asian countries. However, the rapid internationalization process of the seventies brought an end to the success of the technology push tactic. The push strategy only works in situations of little competition. With increased competition, this strategy often leads to fantastic products ending up in ultra-niche markets of "early adopters" with high disposable incomes, but relatively few with clients. Under the push strategy, many American-designed and -produced consumer electronics were quickly put out of business by the Japanese competition.

A second, excellent example is the way the Philips organization had always struggled with the marketing of products such as CDs and DVDs. The cynics used to say, "Philips creates and Sony sells." That Sony could "sell" had to do with the fact that the Japanese tend to be oriented completely from the clients' point of view. Their extreme market-pull approach has its limits too, because the clients often have no idea as to what they want or what is possible.

A different reaction to this dilemma became clear in the different leadership styles of the successive helmsmen at Philips. After a period of time with internally oriented Timmer as leader, Boonstra, an externally oriented marketing man, came along. Finally, Philips had both technology and marketing "in-house." The question was how to connect them. This process is now fully under way under the servant-leadership of Kleisterlee.

Laurent Beaudoin of Bombardier, mentioned earlier, also dealt with a similar issue of internal versus external orientation. He used humility, listening, and patience to get to know the companies that Bombardier had acquired, in order to build on their strengths. He created a strategy that not only reconciled the new acquisitions (internal drive) but also respected the integrity of the acquired companies (external drive). He let the different companies share their dreams so that he could better understand what was possible and whether they were in a state to realize the desired results. The solution of these contrasting proficiencies is just as much about following the acquisition path as it is about respectfully leading what you have acquired. This is the path of the acquiring scholar: a continual learning process, from which to leverage one's efforts.

Internal Business Perspective Versus Client Perspective

Robert Kaplan and David Norton's Balanced Scorecard[1] is justifiably popular. This organizational model shows the balance in a good-functioning organization of several perspectives: financial, customer, internal processes and learning, and group perspective. These categories are also viewed in terms of their relationship to each other. Useful as this model is, it is worth noting that the idea of "balance" seems to be out of place when innovation and learning can result in better financial results, or where internal business processes can reflect the changing directions that the clients wish to go. The word *balance* suggests that the profit that is made in a particular segment is at the cost of another segment. This is not necessarily so. Innovative use of human resources can lead to better and more dynamic strategies, which lead to more consumer satisfaction, which in turn leads to more turnover and, thus, the opportunity for shareholders to reinvest.

Codevelopment

The servant-leader understands that to create a sustainable result it is necessary to improve internal processes by involving the client. Codevelopment programs, where suppliers strategically align themselves with their clients, are an excellent example of this. Applied Materials, a large chip manufacturer, is one company that has effectively used this approach. Its existence is completely dependent on the codevelopment of systems with AMD and Intel. This departs somewhat from the idea of "balance" in the Balanced Scorecard. Where the Balanced Scorecard assumes that value is added by scoring high on each of the four perspectives, Applied Materials believes in creating a win-win situation through the mutual integration of values of the past and future, and from the internal and external values. (See Figure 11.4.)

The servant-leader is helped by an *Integrated Scorecard* to overcome the linear limitation of the Balanced Scorecard.

Bang & Olufsen also rose to the challenge to get insights into the evolving market in order to use this knowledge to remodel its products. The problem was that creativity and technical expertise had dominated the company's attention, while it had lost sight of development costs and commercial aspects.

The board members of Bang & Olufsen formulated the dilemma as follows:

Figure 11.4 Internal process versus external clients

On the one hand, a disconnection of Sales and Marketing both from R&D and from Production and, on the other, the elevation of the latter functions to a dominant position, so that commercial marketing considerations were largely ignored.[2]

CEO Anders Knutsen regarded this imbalance as so serious that he appointed himself the head of Marketing and Sales until he found a vice director with international experience. In this role, he discovered things that the company had ignored for far too long. Bang & Olufsen thought that communication was a one-way process and that its customers were the dealers, not the end users. He recalled: "Naturally, the dealers passed on our arrogant approach to the final client." It turned out that the dealers were using the aura of Bang & Olufsen to improve their own image, while they spent more energy selling the cheaper products better suited to the market, like Philips, Daewoo, Sony, and Grundig. "The product and its market were completely detached," he said. "We needed to get our people thinking in business terms, without sacrificing their pride in their creativity and their products."

Taking Charge Versus Adaptation

A variant of the push-pull dilemma is that of taking charge versus adaptation. Should leaders courageously plow through the waves as the *Titanic* did, or spend their energy avoiding icebergs and anticipating dangers? In other words, is your starting point about taking charge (push) or adaptation (pull)?

The Japanese are masters of adapting. In fact, during the late seventies and eighties, Japanese managers called themselves the "white-water men," a term that typifies the external orientation of the Japanese. At that time, the country was absorbed in competing with the capitalistic system—a system that was invented somewhere else and completely alien. Still, they were rapidly able to make the Western strategy their own and quickly began to make money by using effective production processes and by improving on Western technologies. This is what convinced Japanese leaders that they were "sailing in white waters." They had launched themselves into the economic tide and tried as best they could to tack between the rocks.

At the other extreme is the Anglo-American tendency to take charge completely. A pitfall for these cultures is the idea that they can control everything. This position is similar to "rearranging the deck chairs on the *Titanic*" (1,10 in Figure 11.5). The ship went down though few passengers could believe it was happening. In fact, several lifeboats were launched only half full before people realized the ship was *really* sinking. In modern business, it is possible to fail because you are so efficient that you cannot keep up with everything else around you.

Being *too* efficient is deadly. In recent years, the European fishing fleet has had to be dramatically reduced. Not because they caught too few fish, but because they were actually catching too many, and the fish populations have been depleted. In a similar way, it is also possible that raising the capacity of a factory will have disastrous results, especially if fifty other companies have also done the same during the same period, resulting in a chronic overcapacity.

Despite the appreciation that internally oriented cultures have for self-determination, they cannot do without flexibility and adaptability. No leader is master of his or her lot in the turbulent ocean if he or she drifts rudderless. Waiting until someone comes and rescues him or her is no solution.

The solution is shown in Figure 11.5.

Compass

Both the Anglo-American internal orientation and the East Asian fatalism can have disastrous results when taken to the extreme. Leaders in the modern economy must remain acutely

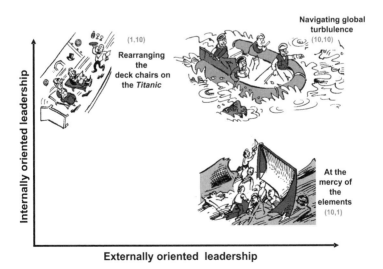

Figure 11.5 Internal-oriented versus external-oriented leadership

aware of the boundaries of their power because business these days is permanently "white-water"; that is, very turbulent and cyclical, and it is only getting worse. From this conviction, servant-leaders act in a cybernetic (Greek for *steersman*) manner. They constantly check their compasses because they realize that unexpected turbulence can move the organization off course and that they need to realign constantly.

Willpower Versus Discretion

In his earlier mentioned book *Good to Great*, Jim Collins offers his vision on the qualities of a successful leader. While he refers to the "level 5 executive," his description is very similar to that of a servant-leader. "The most powerful transformational leaders have access to a paradoxical mixture of willpower and discretion. They are shy and merciless. They are scarce and they cannot be stopped," according to Collins.

The servant-leader combines internally and externally directed powers in unlimited ways. Jim Collins lists the following:

Personal discretion	Professional willpower
• Demonstrates a contagious modesty; avoids public media • Acts in a calm and focused manner • Channels ambition in the organization, not him- or herself; ensures excellent succession • Looks in the *mirror* when something goes wrong and will not blame others	• Achieves excellent results • Directs everything toward long-term results • Sets uncompromising standards for a sustainable, results-driven organization and does not settle for less • Looks out of the *window* to explain the success and thanks destiny and others

Conclusion

Servant-leaders are competent in connecting the mirror and the window (see preceding table) with each other. Precisely how this is done is dependent on the culture. In internally oriented cultures, determination will be the starting point, after which that trait is placed in the service of modesty. Externally oriented cultures prefer to depart from a discreet attitude, to achieve on the basis of pure resolve. The dilemma is the same for all cultures. What differs is the place where you enter the circle.

Resolution

But what should Peter Webber do with all of this? What is an appropriate reaction to the resistance between technological push and market pull? As a servant-leader, he should use the fantastic market knowledge of the southern European and African countries to improve internal processes. Thereafter, he should use the efficient internal processes, which lead to lower costs, in order to serve the client better.

In the next round of personal reviews, he could ask the northern Europeans, "What have you done with the SAP implementation to serve our clients better?" and "What have you done with the client so that the SAP implementation was improved?" Through servant-leadership, the outside world serves the inside world and vice versa.

We Say Good-Bye to Peter Webber

Throughout each of the dilemmas, we have followed Peter Webber and his company as Peter learned to reconcile the dilemmas in his capacity as a servant-leader. Neither Peter's problems nor his solutions are unique—except for the framework that he used (that of dilemma reconciliation) and the approach (that of a servant-leader). Companies all over the world are facing similar dilemmas, and people at every level within organizations, from the work floor to the management board, are putting the principles of servant-leadership into practice. With these tools, we wish Peter well as he continues to navigate the stormy seas of business in the ever-increasing complexity of a global market, and we wish you, the reader, success and productive resolutions as well. In the next part we provide more tools to enable you to start working on your own servant-leadership capabilities.

Notes

1   Robert Kaplan and David Norton, "The Balanced Scorecard: Measures That Drive Performance," *Harvard Business Review* (Boston: Harvard Business Review Press, 1992).
2   Fons Trompenaars and Charles Hampden-Turner, *21 Leaders for the 21st Century* (Oxford: Capstone Publishing, 2001), 144–146.

PART III

Getting Started with Servant-Leadership: A Systematic Approach

From the previous chapters, it is clear that servant-leadership is the most effective model in an intercultural context. Servant-leaders have the ability to not get lost in a quagmire of clashing cultures.

There are many different thoughts about leadership. Some think that "you either have it or you don't." If that were really the case, there is little hope for those people who "haven't got it." Experience teaches us, however, that there are some born leaders, but leadership, and specifically servant-leadership, can definitely be developed. The same thing goes for organizations: by focusing on developing certain processes and systems, it is possible to unveil dilemmas and to create a "reconciling or servant organization."

Developing people and organizations in the direction of servant-leadership is exactly what keeps the Greenleaf Center for Servant-Leadership, as well as Trompenaars Hampden-Turner (THT), busy. Until recently the focus at THT was on the question of the competence of a servant-leader to reconcile differences. Today, there is good insight into the qualities that are effective in intercultural environments, and attention has been shifted to the next question: How can you connect these qualities with better performance and competitive advantage, through the implementation of servant-leadership?

The Internet is used intensively to research this, by gathering information about participants of various workshops. The codification and analysis of more than 8,000 dilemmas that leaders deal with has led to interesting insights. An example of this is the "Golden Dilemmas." The Golden Dilemmas are those that enable us to chart the effectiveness of the leader and the organization. Even more interesting, with this analysis, it is possible to predict the effectiveness of leaders and organizations.

Extensive analysis of this research material has shown that the essential talent of a servant-leader to reconcile dilemmas is not a simple question of nurture or nature. Servant-leadership requires a systematic approach. The whole organization needs to offer people something that supports, inspires, and eases the reconciling of opposites.

It is quite telling that some high-potential individuals made it no further than a compromise (lose-lose), because their working environment did not value creative solutions. On the other hand, it has been found that less efficient individuals became good at reconciling because they were stimulated by their environment to do so.

The main question is: How can someone create a similar environment? It starts with servant-leaders consistently doing what they say. In addition, it is important to create reward systems for individuals and teams that do this as well.

In the end, it is all about the combination of opposing values. This goes hand in hand with the creation of an optimal work environment, which, in turn, leads to a better work culture and becomes embedded in a continuous process so that it becomes a way of life rather than a conceptual exercise.

CAN WE MEASURE INTEGRITY?

The concept of a servant-leader is a fascinating one. Many great people have exemplified this form. Despite their diversity, they had one thing in common: through their behavior they displayed a profound integrity.

Socrates explained during his trial:

> *I only go about telling you all, young and old, not to concern yourselves with your persons and your properties, but to think chiefly of the greatest good of the soul [psyche]. I teach that virtue is not given by money, but that from virtue there comes money and many other good things in life, public and private. If that is the doctrine that corrupts the youth, then my influence is ruinous indeed! But I know that I will not change my ways—not if I have to die many times.*[1]

"I am the king's good servant," insisted Sir Thomas More, "and if that is not enough to keep a man alive I long not to live."[2]

"We must be servants of the poor," said Mahatma ("Great Soul") Gandhi.

A few hours before Martin Luther King Jr. was assassinated, he told his followers:

> *We've got some difficult days ahead. Some worry about what might happen to me from some of our sick, white brothers. But I'm not worried about that now . . . longevity has its place. But He's taken me to the mountaintop and I've seen the promised land. I may not get there with you, but we, as a people, will get to the promised land.* [3]

It was Nelson Mandela who often repeated, "My imprisonment symbolizes our cause and serves my people."

The servant-leader is of course a paradox and thereby represents a dilemma. It is a form of "psychic crucifixion" between two opposed values, symbolic not just of Christianity but the human condition in general. When Jesus died, the Temple curtain tore in half. Losing one's life and saving it is a single process, as is descending only to rise again. This is integrity of the highest order.

It is not easy to measure such a dual concept, but it can be done.

Where Should One Begin with the Implemention of Servant-Leadership?

Few people would fundamentally disagree with the description of servant-leadership above. However, this small minority would say that, just like Peter Webber, they are challenged by having to work with specific goals and practical applications and that nice words only go so far.

Are there some practical tips about how to start introducing servant-leadership into an organization? Definitely, the first point being that it is best to start with yourself, regardless of your position in the company. In addition, it is handy to follow the relatively abstract advice of Plato: "There is nothing more practical than a good theory."

In classic antiquity, Plato formulated four principles that form the basis for a good life: wisdom, courage, moderation, and justice. Servant-leadership goes right back to this tradition. Let's look at the four principles in terms of practical advice for managers.

Wisdom

Plato was one of the most famous philosophers in ancient Greece and he introduced the philosophical term "the love of truth." This philosophy requires that servant-leadership is implemented in an organization in an intelligent manner and is presented in a good way to everyone from the board of directors to management and all the way to the individuals and teams themselves. It is wise to take a systematic approach from the top down, and keep in mind that, wherever you are in an organization, there are many "tops." Start simply with your own "top."

A very practical starting point is to know clearly what the vision—including "higher goal" and mission—of the organization is. In addition, another sign of wisdom is to make a diagnosis of the state of the organization and to make a business case for servant-leadership. It is not a coincidence that Plato used the dialogue as a philosophical method in order to get to the heart of the truth by bringing different points of views together. In practical terms, this means that you start by creating an overview of the organization's most important business dilemmas, like the various ones we have presented in this book. Without an awareness of the dilemmas' tension at play, the need for servant-leadership won't be recognized or felt.

Courage

Servant-leadership requires not only commitment but also the ability to make yourself vulnerable—vulnerability is the highest form of courage. In practical terms, it shows courage when a leader is open to what the employees have to say. How do they see the situation? The first thing a servant-leader will do in order to try to find ways that lead to resolving dilemmas is, wisely, to ask questions. Questions also help servant-leaders to see in which ways they can help others to reconcile their dilemmas. There is also a Dilemma Reconciliation Process (DRP), which was developed to aid the leader in transforming weaknesses into strengths. It is a six-step process that ensures that servant-leaders can transform the dilemma tension into creative energy. In this way courage is connected with caution.

Moderation

However, no one gains if you overdo it. As the saying goes, "Everything is healthy, in moderation." Therefore, moderation is also an important principle. An overdose of servant-leadership runs the risk that employees will soon have had enough and start looking for the next leadership principle. Moderation is another demonstration of wisdom.

In practice, the introduction of servant-leadership means that people also need to become directed on a number of "focal points"—to put 90 percent of their energy into 10 percent of the possibilities. This also goes for choosing which dilemmas have priority when the various dilemmas start to surface. Some companies have more to gain by changing their rewards system than by investing energy in a new advertising campaign. Other organizations are more responsive to changes in the evaluation system than a change in organizational structure. A servant-leader finds precisely what the "sensitive spots" of an organization are, as well as those of the employees, and will focus on them.

Justice

Finally, justice is also necessary. This characteristic plays a role especially in teams where there are people who are not completely "on board" with the principles of servant-leadership. When you have, as a leader, done everything worldly possible to convince people to cooperate, without success, then it is sometimes necessary to part ways. That goes not only for subordinates but also for those on every level. As Jim Collins wrote in his book *Good to Great*, "Show people the door." And take good care of them as they leave.

Justice also applies to openness in terms of communication during a change process. There is no place for political agendas. People need to speak straight, rather than "beat about the bush." A servant-leader has an advantage if he or she can succeed in creating a culture where people speak openly and encourage each other to improve.

Therefore, in summary, the basic steps that someone can take in starting the creation of a servant-leadership process are:

1 Define a vision, mission, and higher goal.
2 Make an inventory of business dilemmas.
3 Determine to what extent servant-leadership is already present.
4 Chart the organizational culture.
5 Start the Dilemma Reconciliation Process.
6 Focus on the most susceptible Processes in the organization.
7 Decide which people will join and which will be asked to leave.
8 Communicate, communicate, communicate!

Notes

1 Plato, *The Apology in the Republic* (apology 30 b0).
2 Robert Bolt, *A Man for All Seasons* (London: Butterworth-Heinemann, 1960).
3 "I See the Promised Land," http://seto.org/king3.html. Taken from *A Testament of Hope: The Essential Writings of Martin Luther King, Jr.*, ed. James M. Washington.

13

BENCHMARKING SERVANT-LEADERSHIP

Servant-leadership means combining the attributes of leadership, in all its pride and prominence, with the attributes of service, in all its humility and self-effacement. But how are we to do this? And how can we measure if we are being successful?

In this regard, it is helpful to first *distinguish* between the two attributes, in order to see how they might be *integrated* thereafter. Only when individuals see that these are highly *contrasting* characteristics does it make sense to see how these might be *unified* by a certain form of leadership.

We, therefore, begin our measurement task with straight-line Likert scales, which, in this case, assess Leadership and Service separately. (See Figure 13.1.) When we do this, our respondents can see that these characteristics differ and that it is first necessary to make a mental distinction.

In Likert's model, choosing one position has consequences for the other. If someone scores 7 on Leadership,

Figure 13.1 Likert scale assessment of leadership and service

for example, then there is only 3 left over for Service. This kind of measurement therefore quickly has limitations because there is no way to measure how integrated values can compound each other.

Part of THT's methodology is to "crack" the line into a two-sided axis, in order to provide a new space in which to envision situations and solutions (Figure 13.2).

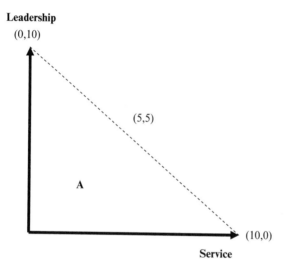

Figure 13.2 Simple two-axes approach

In the above mentioned "linear approach" a score can never come above the diagonal line—between (0,10) and (10,0). The sum of all positions always come out as 10 (7 and 3, 4 and 6, etc.).

The advantage of a representation with two axes is that there is room for a score higher than 10: a creative merging of both positions is possible outside triangle A. (See Figure 13.3.) If you reach a score over the diagonal line (i.e., in triangle B), then we can speak of some integration or *reconciliation*.

Once the axis has been cracked, the space between the two axes is filled in with a grid upon which the position of a leader or an organization can be plotted (Figure 13.4).

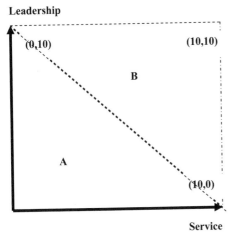

Figure 13.3 Extended two-axes approach

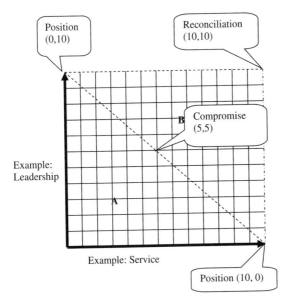

Figure 13.4 Servant-leadership measurement grid

We encourage you to transfer your earlier Likert answers to the grid instrument and reconsider your scores, to see if the two values of Leadership and Service have been *polarized* at top left and bottom right (10, 0 or 0/10), *compromised* in the middle (5/5), *reconciled* at top right (10/10), or now positioned somewhere else on the grid.

Interactive Online Instrument

By means of an interactive diagnotics tool we invite readers to plot out different leadership value tensions as they occur in their own work situation for themselves, or to determine if—or to what extent—there are aspects of servant-leadership present in their own organization. Pop-up balloons that show up on the grid will lead you through the process.

If you wish to use this diagnostic tool to explore your own current situation, you are invited to go to the following link and enter the password as shown.

Website: thtconsulting.com
Password: servant-leader

APPENDIX

Meet the Authors

In this book, Fons Trompenaars and Ed Voerman make a connection between two things that are close to their hearts: dilemma reconciliation and servant-leadership. Because servant-leadership is deeply rooted in practice, they want the reader to begin immediately, giving him or her clear ways to use the concepts in real life. In order to do this, they make use of a servant-leadership instrument from the start: the dialogue. Ed Voerman gets things started by asking his coauthor about his motivation.

Ed: Hey, Fons, what is it about this subject that gets you all fired up?

Fons: What I like so much about servant-leadership, Ed, is that this leadership principle offers extremely practical solutions to universal problems that are faced by people all over the world. An example: Imagine that you are riding in a car with a friend who is speeding and he hits a pedestrian. You are the only witness. What will you do when you are standing in front of the judge? Will you lie for your friend or tell the truth? Everyone wants to help his or her friends and everyone wants to tell the truth. The dilemma is therefore universal, but the way in which people from different cultures deal with this is completely different. It continues to be a challenge to find a solution that brings the various points of view together in such a way that the end result is even better than could have been thought of with either extreme. By making this connection, this reconciliation, you create new things.

Ed: I completely agree with you there, Fons. Above all, what attracts me in servant-leadership is the connecting power. This view can build bridges between people with totally different backgrounds and ideas. Whereas religion in such a situation can act as a divider, because it focuses on the differences, servant-leadership acts as a binder, looking at what people have in common. Listening and being receptive to others are therefore fundamental concepts.

Fons: What have you noticed in your practice?

Ed: During my last trip to China, it became very clear that preparation and putting yourself in the others' shoes are becoming increasingly important for entrepreneurs in the international market. Without this knowledge, misunderstandings easily pop up when you, as a Westerner, do business with your Chinese business partner. This is also why the Chinese have no idea why Americans bring a whole slew of lawyers to the first meetings. In their opinion, this is the wrong order, since they must first make sure there is nothing wrong with the Qing and Li before going further. In order to be able to deal with people in ways that are acceptable to them, you must be able to put yourself in their shoes. Is that something you recognize?

Fons: Yes, definitely. Trompenaars Hampden-Turner functions as a microcosm in this regard. We have people working with us from eight different cultures. There can be culture clashes as a result—and serious ones at that. We deal with the cultural dilemmas on a daily basis.

Ed: For example?

Fons: Communication styles are totally different. One prefers to be direct, another indirect. There are those that can say, with a charming smile, the worst things, while others hold it in, even if they are really upset. We have one person from an Eastern culture who sees everything integrally, as a part of a greater whole. This sometimes clashes with the Anglo-Saxon need for specificity.

Ed: Let me guess how you deal with that. You try to search for the complementarities, with respect for the diversity of your employees. In this case, you map out the bigger picture before going into detail.

Fons: Have you already read this book? But yes, you are right. Looking for solutions at this level is absolutely dependent on respect—you could even say: on love.

Ed: Does this excite all your employees?

Fons: Every once in a while this theory is not used in practice. Very seldom are there people who don't practice what we preach but, when it does happen, that is the time to demonstrate strong leadership; in the words of Jim Collins, it's time to "get the wrong people off the bus, and get the right people in the right seats." You owe that to the rest of your team.

Such a situation is a clear example of the dilemma of "parts versus the whole." Not so long ago we had a couple of very good people working for us who did not fit into our culture. Then, you can either plod on or cut your losses and decisively say good-bye to each other, but in both cases, you lose something. Instead of that, we chose to reconcile the differences on a higher level, and these people became freelancers. In the words of Jim Collins, "they have been kicked off the bus, but they are bicycling quite enthusiastically next to it."

Ed: That also demonstrates that servant-leadership is definitely not a soft model. Like James Autry, a servant-leader from the beginning, you have to have the guts to say: *I love you, but you're fired.*

Fons: That's right. Sometimes you have to be hard because that is the best way you can serve the others. It is important that people commit themselves to the corporate culture. Servant-leadership is not gratuitous.

Ed: Even more important, it is something that informs your whole existence. Servant-leadership is more than a management style. It is a lifestyle, which means that it doesn't stop the moment you step out of the office. Attitude and behavior must be consistent. You cannot be someone different at work from who you are at home.

Fons: Yes you can! There are a lot of people who are popular, understanding, and wonderful bosses at work, but when they are home with their wife, they transform into *grumpy old men* because they used up all of their energy.

Ed: That is true, but then we are not talking about servant-leaders. A servant-leader is the same whether at home or at work, precisely because you can't, at

will, switch "on" and "off" a way of life. It is important that you take the principles that you abide by at
work and use them at home.

Fons: I would even say, *especially* in your family!

Ed: Why?

Fons: Because your family is above everything. I was almost
in a plane crash once. We were flying in especially bad
weather, above the ocean, and suddenly a cloud of
smoke flooded the cabin. There was an announce-
ment that there was some sort of problem with the
electric circuit and, because of this, the lights had to
be turned off. We would also need to make an emer-
gency landing—only we couldn't because we were
over the ocean. So the plane turned around, but the
first chance we had to land was after more than an
hour of flying. That was a very long hour. And the
only thing I could think about during the whole time
was my family. Something like that makes your pri-
orities suddenly very clear.

Ed: You have three children. Could you also apply your
dilemma theory in rearing them?

Fons: The theory is *from the very beginning* suited for
child rearing because, especially in families, you have
opposing values and yet you have to stay with each
other and figure something out. Unlike with employees, when you have a conflict with children, you cannot send them on their way. Therefore, you have to
search for a solution. Servant-leadership is perfect for
that. And the best part of parenting is that it comes
so naturally. You do nothing other than serve your
children.

Ed: Can you elaborate?

Fons: A dilemma that often comes up is the one between rules and exceptions. Bad behavior is usually an exception to a rule. The way in which parents react to the mistakes made by their children says a lot about their servant-leadership abilities. Do they deal with their children strictly, or do they see the mistake as a chance for improvement?

This dilemma occurs on another level. Every child is unique and deserves to be handled in a special way. On the other hand, there has to be rules; otherwise you have anarchy. Thus, you are forever busy looking for rules that apply to all your children, while at the same time consciously making exceptions when the situation calls for it. And you then use these exceptions to make the rules better.

Ed: Some rules work for one child and not at all for another.

Fons: That's right, and there's nothing wrong with that. It is only of concern if a rule doesn't work for any of the three. In that case, you have to take a critical look at the rule.

Ed: Nice theory. But what does that mean in practice?

Fons: Take drugs, for example. I believe in an informative approach. You can forbid your children to smoke until they are 18 and promise them a car in return, but I think it is better to give them the facts about what happens when they smoke. We have always told our children what the consequences are for their behavior and for their choices. By giving them this information, we give the possibility to freely choose for themselves. In this way, you encourage responsibility. *But enough about me.* How is servant-leadership working for you at home, Ed?

Ed: Attitude and behavior must be the same whether at work or at home. Therefore, at home I serve my wife and children. Leading is not a question of playing the boss; instead, it is knowing which moments to set the direction, and which moments to take the direction of my partner. In a family, serving and leading are constantly changing places. You can see it as a kind of two-headed leadership.

Fons: That is therefore the same as with the tango: the man leads where the lady wants to go. Isn't that the essence of leadership?

Ed: Yes, but then you need to know where they want to go! The most important task of a servant-leader is to identify and fulfill the needs of others. That starts with listening. You have to know what moves the others, what their question is—even when they don't ask the question explicitly. If you don't listen to what is needed, then you come up with the wrong solutions. I have seen this in Colombia when I was living and working there. Western volunteers noticed that the villagers' huts were always full of smoke because they cooked inside over open fires. As a result, there were specialists flown over from Holland to come and build chimneys in every hut; and afterwards, this initiative was celebrated with much fanfare. When I returned to the village a year later, every chimney had disappeared. The residents had torn them down because they had a lot of trouble with infestations ever since the chimneys were built. The smoke inside the huts had worked as a deterrent to insects and other infestations, but none of the volunteers had taken the time to ask them "why" they used the current methods. They just placed their own viewpoint onto another culture where it did not fit.

Fons: I could have made a similar mistake when I first started my career. It is a long learning process.

Ed: What was your most important lesson?

Fons: Looking for connections and harmony became second nature. Sometimes we have serious discussions internally, and I notice that in such situations I listen more than I used to. Besides that, I am ever more aware of the necessity to behave consistently. You can say what you want but, in the end, what is most important is what you do. Your behavior has to be clear and just. That doesn't mean, by the way, that I now have the feeling that I have achieved a state of wisdom. As I get older, I realize more and more how much I don't know. Constructive doubt, I like to call it.

Ed: What does that mean for your leadership, Fons?

Fons: I think that over the years I have strengthened my ability to lead and serve, but slowly I am leaning in the direction of serving. I secretly like to have the driver's wheel because I like to have everything under control. But I am consciously trying to let that go.

Ed: Where do you see that?

Fons: It gives me a real sense of satisfaction when I'm working on a new project with a client and he says, "You don't have to come yourself. Just send one of your colleagues." There is nothing easier than always putting yourself forward, but as a leader, it is good to consciously step aside. On the one hand, that makes you feel vulnerable because you don't have the control in your own hands; on the other hand, it is also fantastic to see how people can grow when they get the chance. It really is a kick when you see the fantastic way that they deliver on such a project. Often you feel even better than if you had done it yourself! And often it's much better than I would have done it. Since we're on the subject of confessions, what was *your* most important lesson?

Ed: I think the profound recognition of cultural programming. We are all deeply formed by our culture, our upbringing, and our studies. All these things have programmed us so that in certain situations, we will react in certain ways. It is an art form to become aware of this and to then let it go so that you can truly be open for what people have to say instead of thinking that you already know it all. Only when you realize that can you learn from others and demonstrate that not only can you have equally valued contact, but also that real communication is possible.

Fons: Too bad that people have to learn this sort of thing the hard way.

Ed: That's why I'm happy that we have tools nowadays that can help people: the Servant-Leadership Academy, for example. Today's leaders have the responsibility to give direction to the next generation. Every generation asks the question again about what is the purpose of existence. That question, however, has long ago been answered: it is to serve others. As well-known psychiatrist Viktor Frankl said: "It is not so important what we expect from life, but more what life expects from *us*." With the foundation of the Servant-Leadership Academy last year, we created a platform where people can learn how to find their way in the world of servant-leadership and their own role therein. This means that a new generation of leaders is coming that has learned how to give the desire to serve others real substance. This will have a positive influence on their environments because they are capable of building bridges and bringing the best out of others. The Academy offers people the chance, together with other like-minded people, to take a journey and fill their suitcases with valuable experience. This journey does not end with a diploma and the end of your learning process. If everything goes right, you will stay on this journey the rest of your life, enjoying all cultural differences and in the end discovering that all people are basically the same.

More information

For more information regarding servant-leadership:
greenleaf.org
servantleadershipcenter.net

For more information regarding Trompenaars Hampden-Turner (THT):
thtconsulting.com

INDEX